D0499865

"The most important books I have read. I study them like a bible!"
Elisabeth Kübler-Ross, M.D., author of *On Death and Dying*.

"These words embody tolerance, universality, love and compassion—hallmarks of all Great Teachings. They turn our attention inward to our own divine nature, instead of diverting it outward. Paul Ferrini is a modern-day Kahlil Gibran—poet, mystic, visionary, teller of truth." Larry Dossey, M.D., author of *Healing Words: The Power of Prayer and the Practice of Medicine*.

"Paul Ferrini leads us skillfully and courageously beyond shame, blame and attachment to our wounds into the depths of self-forgiveness. His work is a must-read for all people who are ready to take responsibility for their own healing." John Bradshaw, author of *Family Secrets*.

"A breath of fresh air in an often musty and cluttered domain. With sweetness, clarity, and simplicity we are directed to the truth within. I read this book whenever my heart directs, which is often." Pat Rodegast, author of *Emmanuel's Book I, II and III*.

"Paul Ferrini's writing is authentic, delightful and wise. It reconnects the reader to the Spirit Within, to that place where even our deepest wounds can be healed." Joan Borysenko, Ph.D., author of *Guilt is the Teacher, Love is the Answer*.

"I feel that this work comes from a continuous friendship with the deepest part of the Self. I trust its wisdom." Coleman Barks, poet and translator.

"Paul Ferrini's wonderful books show a way to walk lightly with joy on planet earth." Gerald Jampolsky, M.D., author of *Love is Letting Go of Fear*.

Book Design by Paul Ferrini
and Lisa Carta

Library of Congress Number
2006920677

ISBN # 1-879159-62-7

Heartways Press
9 Phillips Street, Greenfield MA 01301
www.heartwayspress.com

Manufactured in the United States of America

THE PRESENCE OF
LOVE

God's Answer to
Humanity's Call for Help

PAUL FERRINI

Table of Contents

Introduction

And I John saw the holy city New Jerusalem
coming down from God out of heaven.
REVELATIONS 21:2

If you have found your way to this book, you are hearing humanity's cry for help in the time of its greatest need. You are being called now to heal at the deepest levels so that you can be an inspiration to others and a witness to the power of love.

You know that what you think, feel, say and do in your life does matter. It will not only shape your personal destiny. It will have an impact on many others.

The challenges the human family faces in the 21st Century —and in the next seven years in particular—are awesome ones. It is easy to feel hopeless or overwhelmed by the number and the magnitude of the problems that must be solved. Many people understandably feel that "what I do will not matter. It won't make a difference."

Nothing, however, could be further from the truth. We human beings created the challenges that we face and we have the capacity to meet them. To do so, however, will require the kind of cooperation the world has never seen. All of us will have to rise above self-interest and learn to serve the common good.

Spirit must be reawakened in the human family: first in our own hearts and then in the hearts of others. Recognizing the need for transforming human consciousness from fear to Love, God and all of Her messengers are busy at work, building an army of Love givers that will restore health and harmony to planet Earth.

Gradually, people will see God's foot soldiers actively uplifting hearts and awakening minds. They will see the houses of healing for the 21st Century steadily being built, as people heal their emotional trauma and become capable of offering love without conditions.

These are exciting times, times when many miracles will occur and we will see the power of love in action. But please understand, none of this would be possible if we had not volunteered for this assignment, because nobody else is going to do it. We are the ones who volunteered and the ones to whom this work has been entrusted.

Coming Face to Face

The human family is at a crossroads now. We can no longer live as we have lived in the past. We can no longer afford to be sloppy, careless, or impulsive with our creations. We need to create compassionately and be responsible for what we create.

This is not something we can leave till tomorrow. We must start right now, each one of us. The choices that we make do matter, for we will reap as we have sown. Individually and collectively, we will see the fruits of our actions in this lifetime.

This is the last generation of human beings who will be able to live on the planet in selfishness and greed. This is the last generation that will be able to pollute the air and the water. If we do not open our hearts to each other and become good stewards for our planet, we will witness the gradual degradation and eventual demise of human life on planet earth.

We are coming face to face with ourselves now. Every thought, every emotion is out-picturing, not just in our private lives, but on the collective screen of consciousness. There is nowhere to hide.

The time for denial is over on planet Earth. Each one of us is responsible for what we think, how we feel, what we say, and what we do. The time for transparency has come, individually and collectively.

Lies and deceptions will no longer be tolerated. Projections must be taken back. We can no longer try to attribute to someone else the thoughts and feelings that belong to us. We can no longer try to make any one else responsible for what we say or do.

The storms that are coming our way are not just external ones. There will be hurricanes, tornadoes and earthquakes in our minds and our hearts. Repressed material will erupt. Secrets will be told. Shame will be exposed and fear will come up for healing. The process of purification has already begun, within us and around us.

This is a time of great energy. It is a time when the potential for healing and transformation is greater than it has ever been before. If we are ready to heal, this is a good thing. If we aren't, it is a scary time to be alive.

The Purifying Fire

Until we open to our healing, it is hard to know the power of love in our lives. But once we crack open—once our defense mechanisms shatter and we come face to face with our fear—something incredible happens. Love comes into the dark places where we used to hide our fear and our shame. It begins to inhabit our emotional body.

A flame is lit that will not go out. It can only grow, illuminating all of the cavernous places within our hearts and minds. It burns and consumes everything except itself. No untruth can stand its heat. No unworthiness can survive its relentless scrutiny.

As the flame flourishes and becomes a roaring fire, we bring a whole new energy and attitude toward our lives. We begin to live in the light of our own self-forgiveness. We begin to live in the warmth of our own compassion.

As the fire of love burns, it becomes a smelting furnace, liquefying even the hardest metals. Our neuroses and resistances are dissolved. Our ego agendas are annihilated. Our shame is eradicated.

As the old world crumbles and falls apart, we begin to build a new world on the planet, brick by brick, stone by stone. New compassionate businesses and institutions arise. They embody the spirit of equality and exist solely for the purpose of serving and empowering human beings.

So let us not dwell on the old buildings that are crumbling around us. Let's not focus on the roles we can no longer play or the work that we can no longer force ourselves to do. Instead, let us focus on what we can create that will work, for us and for others.

Creating a New World Together

The world that we will create together will be a very different world than the one that we have now. It will not be a fear-driven, shame-based world, but a world based on acceptance and love. It will not be a world where we are afraid to face our pain and afraid to feel the pain of others. It will be a compassionate world that will recognize our wounds and help us heal from them. It will be a world where we can be profoundly honest and present with each other, an authentic world, in which each of us is empowered to be who we are and to express our creative gifts.

Let's not waste time and energy despairing that this new world has not yet taken shape. The seeds are sown. The saplings are springing up. We need to take up the watering can and tend to them.

Our work of love is calling to us. Our gift is needed. Without it, the world cannot be lifted up out of darkness.

In Revelations, we are told that a New Jerusalem will be born, a shining city built out of the ashes of the crumbling world. That is the city we are building together.

It does not matter that only a few of us know how to read the blueprints, dig the trenches and get the foundation in. We don't need the framers yet. They have been given notice and will arrive when we are ready for them. And the plumbers, the electricians, and the finish carpenters will not be far behind.

Welcome to the Golden Temple Brigade! Your resume was impressive. Now let's see what you can do.

Namaste. I bow to the Spirit within you.

Paul Ferrini
Parrish, Florida
Christmas, 2005

A Note on The Spiritual Mastery Series

This book is Part Three of my *Course in Spiritual Mastery*. The first two volumes in the Spiritual Mastery Series—*The Laws of Love* and *The Power of Love*—present us with 10 spiritual principles and 10 spiritual practices that can guide our growth as we learn to heal our wounds and step into our full empowerment as teachers, healers and leaders in the new millennium.

To read a summary of the contents of the previous two *Mastery* books, turn to Appendix 1. To obtain the full benefit of the *Course,* I suggest that you read the other two books in the series and begin working with the 10 principles and practices. However, you can feel free to read this third book first if you are drawn to it.

Trust the intuition that led you to open this book. You would not be knocking on this door if you were not ready to enter.

Please note that workbook lessons for Spiritual Mastery *students for this chapter and the next nine chapters can be found in the Appendix 3.*

PART ONE

Hearing the Call

I

The Presence of Love

This presence of love
that begins in your heart
is so great it contains universes.
It gives life to all and sustains all
with its perpetual gifts.

The Breath of Life

Please, join me now and take a deep breath. As you exhale, let go of all the thoughts you have in your head. Just let them fall away with the breath. And, as you breathe in, open your heart to this moment. Know that now is unique, unpredictable, indeed miraculous.

As you breathe, let go of the person you thought you were. Let go of all of the experiences you bring with you. Just breathe and be in your absolute purity and simplicity. Be the breath. Be the light in which things are seen. Be the silence in which sound registers.

Be the background, the container, the canvas on which life paints itself. Be receptive. Be open.

Know now, in this moment, that all the love that you have been seeking through other people and outer experiences already abides in your heart. Feel the warmth of that love as it abides with you.

That is *the presence*. It has no beginning or end. It is ubiquitous and omnipresent. It exists always and everywhere. There is no place where this love is not.

Feel that holy presence in your heart. It is the Grail, the cup of grace. As you commune with it, the cup is filled to the brim and overflows the rim. There is so much love there. No cup can contain it.

It flows like a great river into the ocean of life, yet even the ocean cannot contain it. Earth is not big enough to hold it, nor is the Solar system or the Milky Way.

This love is so great it cannot be contained. So do not try to hold onto it. Let it flow out of you to everyone in your experience. Let it wrap around your parents and your children. Let it embrace your community, your country, your planet.

Let it surround all things. Let it be the container in which you live, move and breathe.

Imagine: this simple, pure presence that begins in your heart is so great it contains universes. Some people call it God or Spirit. Some call it the Great Mother. It gives life to all and sustains all with its perpetual gifts.

That is the nature of love. That is the indwelling presence that embraces all things. That is where we begin.

A Simple Truth that will Change your Life

And now understand me, dear ones. There is only one thing that you need to grasp and most of the suffering you experience will disappear from your life.

"What is that?" you ask.

It is simply this: neither the past nor the future exists. They have no existential validity.

Past and future are just stories we invent to try to create safety and predictability in our lives. Unfortunately, we get lost in the stories and spend our lives defending them. In our attempt to protect ourselves from change, we create a very limited experience of life.

"But what is the alternative?" you ask.

The alternative is to let your experience be what it is in any moment. Do not try to make it go away. Do not try to hold onto it.

Just allow life to unfold on its own timetable in its own unique way. That way you stop trying to take charge of your life and you stop closing the door to the possibilities that abound around you.

As you stop pulling the past along with you, your burden becomes lighter. You have a freedom you did not have before. It is the freedom to be present without expectations or regrets. You reclaim the present moment in your life. And that is an ecstatic experience, because that is where you meet life directly and profoundly.

Each moment is fresh, new, innocent, spontaneous and you are called to dance with it. Such a dance has no beginning or end. It simply is, in all its changing magnificence.

If, instead, we attempt to direct the cosmic dance, we are bound to be frustrated. We cannot even direct ourselves, never mind direct the will of creation. Let us be humble here. We know so little about anything. Why would we take on the direction of the wind and the motion of the stars?

It is easier and more effective to allow ourselves to be swept up by the current of life than to try to engineer its direction or its rate of flow. Those who try to push the river usually fall in kicking and screaming and a few might not make it back to the riverbank.

So, my friends, again let us take a deep breath and let it go. We are not here to push the river or try to hold it back. We are here to sit under the oak tree on the riverbank until the river calls us and, when it does, to surrender to the current and let it take us where it will.

There are far greater forces at work here than our little will. Let us trust them. And let us let go into that trust.

The Power of not Knowing

As long as you are trying to direct your life or the lives of others, you have the burden of knowing or the embarrassment of not-knowing. When you give up all that, not knowing becomes a freedom and a blessing.

It is like a man who has a closet full of suits. He has to clean them and press them. He has to wear the right kind of jacket with the right kind of shirt and tie. He needs a different pair of shoes for each outfit. Meanwhile, over the years, his wardrobe grows. Eventually, he needs several large rooms just to house his clothes.

It takes a lot of energy to be fashionable and well dressed. You can spend a lifetime doing it and some people do. But when the man finally realizes that clothes are not necessary, he can just discard them and move to a smaller house. He can simplify his life. He can move closer to the river. He doesn't even need a bathing suit to jump into the water.

Whereas before he spent hours thinking about what he was going to wear or how he was going to look, now he has time to play his flute and watch the birds fly by overhead. He leaves behind his stressful life for the ecstatic life of living in the moment.

The same, my friends, is true of the garments of the mind. Our thoughts and the emotions attached to them keep us very busy. Sometimes they even keep us awake at night. But when we recognize the mechanical nature of thought and the ego structure it supports, we can begin to surrender it.

We do not do it with anger or with fear. Indeed, it must be done gently. We can't make thinking or trying to control bad or wrong, or we will be trying to overcome the ego with the ego. And that never works.

So we don't beat ourselves up for our attachment to words and concepts. We just recognize their limitation and then gently put our thoughts aside so that we can stay open to the presence of love in our hearts. That is our simple practice. We recognize that we don't know anything, put our ego-agenda aside, and just fall into the heart.

The more we breathe and dwell in the heart, the more we

stop focusing on the past or the future, the more we become aware of new possibilities. We fully inhabit the moment and open to its abundance.

This represents our return to the Garden, our return to innocence, our return to our original nature. It means that we are going to shift from working out of sacrifice to joyful work. It means that we are going to move out of struggle and into grace.

We stop filling up the space-time continuum with our incessant building and other fear-driven activities. We learn to let things be as they are. And so we re-discover sacred space and time. We make room for miracles.

The whole field of possibility opens to us. Creativity and inspiration abound. We do not walk, talk or make love the way we did before.

Not being attached to what we think we know, we are free to learn and to grow. Our lives unfold with greater emotional richness and sensitivity, and we live, not as oppressors or occupiers, but as lovers.

Perhaps you think I am painting the picture of some unrealizable utopia. I am not. I am saying that this is what is possible right now. Indeed, it is only possible now, in this moment.

Are you willing to breathe into these possibilities? Are you willing to let the past go and let the future take care of itself? Are you willing to give the stewardship of your life back to God and her angels?

You see, yesterday was too early and tomorrow will be too late. Now is the only time that peace is possible.

2

The Call to Awaken

Behold, I stand at the door, and knock.
If any man hear my voice, and open the door,
I will come in to him,
and will sup with him, and he with me.

REVELATIONS 3:20

The Embodiment of the Divine Energy

Time is ripe for change on planet earth and you and I are going to play an important role in bringing that change forward. God needs many helpers and you and I are being called to help in our unique way. Of course, being called is not always a comfortable process. Sometimes, we pull away and refuse to answer the call, hoping that it will go away.

But it doesn't. Indeed, for most of us, it just gets louder and more disturbing. Until we answer the door, the pounding and the ringing will continue.

A year ago, as I was driving in my car to South Florida, my

body was flooded by light. I felt a burning all through my body. It started in my heart and spread through my arms and legs. It permeated every cell in my body.

I expected it to go away, but it did not. It continued to burn and intensify. After a while, I realized I could not contain the energy. I had to share it with someone, anyone. I called a friend and asked her if I could share this energy with her. I had no idea what would happen. I allowed the energy to flow through my hands to her and, to my amazement, she was able to feel in her own heart the same fiery energy that was in mine.

This energy could not only be embodied. It could be transmitted.

***

Many years ago, when I first began working with the Christ energy, I had a dream. I was in a cave somewhere in the Middle East. There were several figures in the cave wearing long brown robes with hoods covering their hair so that you could see only their faces. One of them rose up and began to approach me looking directly into my eyes. I looked into those eyes and I knew them. They were the eyes of Jesus.

"You will heal," he told me "as I heal" and he made several gestures without speaking, pointing first to his third eye, then to his heart, and then extending his hands toward me. I understood immediately the meaning behind the gestures. The head represented the teaching of truth, which is simple and uncomplicated.

"One must have a conviction about the absolute worthiness and innocence of the person," he inferred. "One must be open here, (he pointed to his heart). One must feel acceptance and compassion. It is a palpable energetic reality." And then, (extending his hands), he said "This is how the energy of mind and heart triangulate and extend through the hands."

The dream was a powerful one and I remembered it when the energy began to embody in me. And I realized that the time had come to begin the healing ministry he had called me to.

***

Like all major events in my life, I didn't have to figure any of this out. It just happened. The energy itself told me that it was time.

When I was fifteen my friend invited me to go to a Quaker meeting. I went reluctantly. I wasn't even sure that I believed in God. So I just sat there patiently waiting for the meeting to be over. And then my chair began to shake and my heart began to pound. Without having any idea about what was happening I felt myself rise to my feet and begin speaking words that spontaneously came into my mind. I guess I must have gone on for twenty minutes or so. I had no idea.

After the service many people came up to me and told me how moving my sharing had been to them. I didn't know what they were talking about because I didn't remember anything I had said.

All my life I have been a mouthpiece for my teachers. I can take no credit for anything that comes through my lips. I exist simply to speak the words that are given to me.

***

Yet it hasn't been easy for me to step forward. When I was twenty-three I went through my dark night of the soul. I was plunged into despair for my own heart and the heart of the planet. Everything outside of me seemed bleak. I got up at 4 AM and road my bicycle through the streets of Cambridge, Massachusetts, shivering in the icy winter air. I pedaled fast to stay warm and eventually arrived at work in Somerville, where I picked up my truck and began my deliveries. The people I delivered to were obviously in pain. They were struggling financially and emotionally, as I was. I felt their pain. I felt my own pain.

When I drove over the bridge by the Museum of Science, the sunrise would arrive in excruciating, heart-rending colors. I was writing a collection of poems entitled "The Thorns of Dawn." I didn't know it then, but I was experiencing my own crucifixion.

I remember sitting at the kitchen table after finishing the last poem, feeling that there was no reason to go on living. And I asked God "Why should I stay?"

I really didn't expect to get an answer.

To my surprise I heard a booming voice in my head say GO INTO THE LIVING ROOM, CLOSE YOUR EYES AND PICK OUT A BOOK FROM THE BOOKCASE.

I had nothing to lose, so I did as I was asked and pulled out a book. It was *I and Thou* by Martin Buber. "Now open the book and begin reading." Again, I complied, and after a couple of sentences I was dumbfounded. These were exactly the words that I needed to hear.

"There were two worlds," Buber wrote: "the world of I - Thou, and the world of I-It." I had experienced the first world of spiritual oneness and connection, but only fleetingly. The second world was the one I lived in most of the time. It was the world of pain and misery, the world of suffering, the world that was empty of meaning or purpose

And then I continued to the next paragraph and received my homework for the rest of my embodiment. "And it is up to you," Buber told me, "which world you choose to see."

From that moment on, I could no longer be a victim of the world. I could no longer complain about the way things were. I had work to do. I had to reclaim the light within my own soul.

And so the process of my atonement began and it continues to this day. Only now it is not just about my connection to oneness. It is about our collective connection to it.

Consciousness on the planet is at a crossroads. We have reached the quantum moment when it is time for us all to wake up. But we cannot do this out of fear. We have to do it out of love, first for ourselves, and then for others.

Let me tell you a story. It is my little Kabalistic story of creation. It goes like this . . .

How God Gave Himself Away

In the time of Creation, the light of God was so great that no one could look at it. God knew this and it troubled Him. So He decided to give away some of His light.

In order to do this, He had to create an opposite, a darkness that could receive His light. So God created the World. And the World was completely dark and impenetrable.

Then God gave to the World a little of His light and a part of the World lit up like a tiny candle in the darkness. Then, He gave some more light and other candles became illumined.

God took great delight giving away His light and watching the sparks of light take root in the darkness. Gradually, the darkness was illumined. Indeed, it could be said that the dark World that God created was filled with millions of sparkling lights.

Of course, the more God gave away His light to the world, the darker He became. Yet He was taking total delight in His giving and He did not notice how He was beginning to fade from sight. In the end, without knowing it, He gave away the last rays of His light. And thus, He became invisible.

Now all that remained of God was the sparks of light burning in the darkness and they did not remember their origin. God had become invested in the world. His light had become embodied.

Now in each one of us, the spark of God's light burns. For some, as for Moses, it is a bush on fire. For others, it is a flaming wick or an ember glowing in the darkness.

Still others of us do not know that this spark lives within us. We feel that we have come into this dark world without hope, without meaning, without a ray of light to guide our way.

We look for God in the skies and all we see are distant stars. We look for God in the eyes of our brothers and sisters and all we see are faces twisted by pain or frozen in resignation.

Of course, we don't know yet that God's light can be found only within our own hearts. Until we find our own light, it is impossible to see the light of others.

But once we see the tiny rays of light that lie hidden in the dark night of our souls, once we learn to say "yes" to ourselves at the deepest emotional level, everything begins to change. We feel God's love in our hearts. We feel the presence and know that we can turn to God when we need to for guidance and support. Wherever we go, we know that God walks with us.

As our light gets stronger, we begin to notice all of the eyes that light up and dance like flames in the darkness. That is the sign that we have accepted our relationship with God. We have accepted our divine origin and our mandate to be a torch, a shining star, a vehicle for the expression of love in the world.

Others cannot help but notice. When they come into our presence, they feel the warmth and the light of our love. They see the spiritual fire burning in our eyes. And, if they look deeply enough, they too catch fire. The fire in one heart calls forth the fire in another. This is the power of Spirit at work in our lives.

And so we learn to celebrate the spark that lives in the hearts of all human beings. God's creation remembers its Creator and the circle of giving is complete. The Light that God gave to us returns to Him through us. This, as you know, is when the Messiah comes, when the hearts and minds of women and men remember God and experience their divinity, when all the separate lights come together into a single light and the world is lifted up out of darkness.

The Call to Awaken

These are important times for our planet and the consciousness on it, times when the prophecies are to be fulfilled, not perhaps as the fundamentalists understand them, but fulfilled nonetheless.

Earth is going through her collective crucifixion, her dark night of the soul, and we are along for the ride. Our choice is a simple one. We can respond in fear or we can respond in love, holding our fears and those of others with gentleness and compassion.

The shift in consciousness that is necessary on our planet cannot be made in fear, nor can it be made by pretending that we are not afraid when we are. It can only be made by making friends with our fear and learning to hold it gently. Then, we become the savior, the bringer of love to our own experience. And that is the moment when we become useful to God. That is the moment when we leave the ego agenda behind and become an instrument of love in a fearful world.

These are powerful times . . . times when you and I are asked to step forward and be the love we have been reading about. The time has come to walk our talk, to put the books down, to bring the energy of love into our hearts and become its embodiment.

To do this we do not have to be perfect, totally healed or enlightened. That is the myth that holds us back!

All that is required is that we accept ourselves as human beings . . . learning from our mistakes . . . forgiving and asking for forgiveness.

Our humanness does not condemn us. In fact, accepting our imperfection and that of others is a necessary requirement for us to step forward into our full empowerment. It's a requirement for learning how to trust in our higher power and our higher purpose.

No, we do not have to be perfect to be a messenger of God. The messenger does not have to have four PhDs or divinity degrees. She just needs to trust the truth that has been given to her and be willing to share it. She doesn't even need to know where to go or what words to speak, because the divine energy within her will guide her footsteps and put the words into her mouth when she opens it.

This Divine Presence that guides us is not the God that is separate from us but the God within our heart of hearts . . . It is our essence . . . It is not the God that judges or punishes us, but the God within that loves and accepts us without conditions.

It is the same God that spoke through Jesus and Buddha and Lao Tzu and Krishna. It is the God of love, the Bodhisattva of compassion. It is the Friend who is always with us.

The Friend . . . such an elegant term . . . Rumi calls Shams the Friend, and so do the Quakers address each other as friends, as equals.

No, our humanity does not condemn us. It prepares us to accept our divinity by helping us cultivate compassion for ourselves and others.

For who is a Christ or Buddha but one who has experienced suffering and felt compassion for the pain of the human experience? Only such a one can become a Christ . . . an anointed one!

One who has never experienced suffering does not qualify. Even Gautama did not qualify until he passed through the gates of his palace and saw the squalor and misery of human experience.

One who has not felt pain, one who has not felt fear, one who has not suffered grief and despair, cannot experience the depth of love and compassion that a Christ or Buddha does. That is why God has a human face; that is why there is a Jesus, a Gautama, a Rumi . . . That is why there is a you and an I.

"But," you ask, "How can we mention our own names along with names of these great masters?" Because we are walking the path that bears their footprints . . . Where they are now . . . we are going . . . each one of us. We are on the road to spiritual mastery.

***

"But who is the master?" you ask. "Is he not the enlightened one, the resurrected one, the one who has conquered pain and fear?"

No. That is the myth. The true master is not one who has conquered pain, but one who has suffered it, let it in, walked with it and allowed it to carve out a sanctuary in her heart. She is not the one who denies fear or tries to make it go away, but the one who invites it in and holds it compassionately.

The true master is not the one meditating on the mountaintop, communing with the angels in the clouds, but the one facing the challenges of life with caring and compassion—like Mother Theresa or Brother Toby . . . caring for the poor, the outcasts of society, the AIDs babies in the orphanages, the ones without food and shelter from the elements, the ones without hope and more pain than they can bear alone.

They and others like them are not doing this to score brownie points in heaven. They are doing this because the greatest bliss, the most profound way to know God in the human experience, is to serve our brother or sister.

The master does not care about what you believe or espouse. She cares about what you do.

Jesus told us we would know a tree by its fruits. What are the fruits of your experience?

***

My friends, the time for a separate, individual spirituality is over. From this moment on we do not heal alone but together.

The energy has shifted.

The call has gone out and each one of you, in one way or another, has heard the call and knows that you have been asked to step forward to play your part in the healing and atonement of consciousness on the planet.

But don't worry. It's no big deal. It has nothing to do with your ego. It's all about the surrender of that ego, the letting go of your unworthiness. For you are worthy and so is everyone else.

Our healing and that of our brothers and sisters is one and the same. We are all in the process of shifting from fear to love and the love that we learn to give to ourselves spontaneously extends to others.

There is no way to love others without first offering that unconditional love to ourselves. There is no way to facilitate healing for others until we begin to heal the wounds in our own emotional body.

None of us are alone in that. This is the work all of us are engaged in.

Many of us hold back, shy away from stepping forward into our life purpose, because we feel we have to be totally healed, but that is not the case. The healing you have already done, you can extend to others. The door you have walked through, you can open for others.

You do not need to make it happen . . . It happens by itself if you are willing. It all comes down to that . . .

Are you willing? If so, you are ready.

Please understand this simple message: You do not have to be ready to be willing. You merely have to be willing! If you are willing, the healing of self and others moves through you and you become an instrument of love. God will use you in the appropriate time and place.

You cannot know what that is about. It is beyond your comprehension. Your job is just to show up. You may not know what to say, but when you show up the words will be given to you. You may not know where to go, but move your feet and the direction will become clear.

The Only True Authority

Human beings only have one authority and it is not the authority of their ego structure. That is a false authority.

The time has come to make friends with our fear, to bring love to the wounded child within us, individually and collectively. As we do that, we come to know the only true authority within human consciousness and experience and that is the authority of love.

No, not conditional love, but love without conditions. Not love for some at the expense of others. But love for all, now and in every moment.

That alone can be trusted . . . anything less than that comes from fear and must be questioned.

Do not make the mistake of turning your life over to an external authority, because no one but you knows what you need in your heart of hearts. Only you know and that is the Holy Grail you must seek.

But do not think that you will find it in the world. It cannot be found there. It can be found only in the inmost sanctuary where you and God come face to face.

That is the place of the supreme mystery. It will always be a mystery. It can be experienced but it cannot easily be described.

Lao Tzu said it clearly, "The truth that can be described is not the real truth." The real truth rests in your heart. No one else can take you to it. Your fear and the collective fear that surrounds you cannot take you there. Only love can lead you there.

My friend Don told me that he spent his whole life waiting for his ship to come in. He finally realized it wasn't coming in. He gave up hope of any outside salvation and that is when everything shifted! That is when he became the ship he was waiting for. That is when he answered his own call for love.

You and I are not unlike Don. We think we are unworthy. We think someone else will answer the call. But then we start hearing that unmistakable knock on the door and it keeps on knocking until we get up and pull the door open.

Then we realize that what we were most afraid of is exactly what we have been praying for all of our lives.

It's ironic is it not? You are the savior. You are the bringer of love. If you can bring it to yourself, you can bring it to all of God's children. For all of God's children are one and the same. All are asking for love and all must answer the call.

***

Let me share a prayer with you. It was a prayer that was written on election day, 2004.

If the words of this prayer resonate with you, please say them and let them inspire you to trust your gift and offer it to the world. For you have come here with an important purpose and a necessary role to play in the atonement of human consciousness on planet earth. You have come to heal and to help build the houses of healing that are necessary for the 21st century.

That is the work you are being called to. And the fulfillment of your life depends on whether or not you answer that call.

Spiritual Mastery Prayer

Father/ Mother God:
Help me to feel my oneness with you
and my equality with my brothers and sisters.

Help me to recognize my judgments
and to look within for correction.

Help me to give up shame and blame
and to learn from my errors
so that I do not repeat them.

Help me to care for my body, my family,
my community and my planet.

Help me to create what is for my highest good
and for the highest good of others.
Help me to be responsible for my creations.

Help me give up victim consciousness
and realize that I am a powerful person
with many creative choices.

Help me to stand up for myself in a loving way
without attacking others or seeking to influence
the choices they need to make.

Help me offer freedom to others
so that I may receive it in return.

Help me reach out with compassion to those in pain,
in grief, under stress, or in limitation of any kind
and offer them hope and encouragement.

Allow my heart to open to them.
Allow my eyes to see beyond the behavior
that is motivated by fear and unworthiness.

May I offer to others and to myself
the unconditional love and acceptance you offer to me.

Help me to master my skills and talents
so that I may place them in your service
and fulfill my purpose here.

Help me to step into the role you would have me play
in inspiring, empowering and uplifting others.

Help me to trust my gifts and give them
without expectation of return
whenever the opportunity arises.

Help me to give freely and love freely
surrendering the outcome to you.

Help me surrender the need to control
so that I can live spontaneously
and with your grace.

Help me to understand and heal my wounds
so that I don't push love away
or block its presence in my heart
and in my relationships.

Help me soften and become vulnerable.
Help me learn to ask for help
and trust the help that you offer me.

Allow me to heal the past
so that I can enter the present fully.

Allow me to become a doorway
for the healing of others
and let me walk courageously through the door
that has been opened for me.

Help me surrender what is false
and establish in what is true
firmly and with conviction.

Help me to walk my talk, listen deeply,
and speak only when I have something helpful to say.

Help me to understand that the Friend
is always with me
and my only purpose is to be a Friend to others.

Help me detach from name and fame
and surrender all forms of external authority
so that I can be guided by the authority within.

Allow me to know at all times and in all places
that the highest good of others
is and will always be my highest good.

Let all that separates me from others fall away
so that I may recognize the One Self in all beings.

Allow me to complete my work on earth
with care and humility
and return to you when my work here is done.

May all veils and barriers that separate us dissolve
so that I may dwell fully and completely
in the heart of your love.

Amen

3
Messages from the Masters

The time has come
for you to shine your light.
It is time for you to arise
and give your gift to the world.

Messages from the Masters

A round the time the energy began to embody in me, I began to receive a series of messages that I was told to get out to people as soon as possible. The endgame scenario had begun on planet Earth, I was told, and we human beings were going to have to face the consequences of the choices that we had made in the past. We were also going to have to learn to become responsible for our present-moment choices and creations.

It was time for the teachers, the healers, and the leaders of the future to step forward and begin to do the work they had signed up for. I was told in no uncertain terms that there was no time to waste.

Those who were being asked to step forward immediately, I was told, would feel the energy in these messages. They would feel a warmth or vibration in their hearts, their hands or feet as they read them. Some would feel it like a fire spreading all though their bodies. These people would be the first wave of spiritual students.

I would work with them and help them to step fully into their power as teachers and healers. And then they would assist me in receiving and training the next wave of students.

At the time of this writing, the first wave is nearly complete in their training and the second wave is beginning to move toward us. The work is intensifying.

Many of you have been reading my words for years, but you have been afraid to shine your light. My friends, your apprenticeship is over. The time has come for you to shine your light and become the teaching. It is time for you to arise and give your gift to the world.

I am here to help you do that.

The following messages speak for themselves. If they resonate in your heart, please acknowledge them and come and join us in this work of personal and planetary transformation. Your gift is needed now.

The Awakening of Love Without Conditions on Planet Earth

Know that this communication comes from the highest intelligence available to the planet right now. It has been sent to you so that you can connect with the higher frequency energies that are needed to transform your life and that of the world in which you live.

As you know, the energies of fear feed off each other. These are old energies that need to be shifted. However, they cannot be shifted within their reactive field of consciousness. Help from the higher frequency energies is necessary.

You are capable of receiving these higher energies if your heart is open and you know that you can no longer live your life through your ego structure.

The Great Mother is reaching out now to bring our planet and the consciousness on it into Her nurturing embrace. Human consciousness is ready for the return to the feminine.

The feminine essence embodies the energy of love without conditions. It has no limits, no boundaries, no exceptions. Everyone may be brought into this circle and lifted up by the higher frequency energies. That is what it means to ascend or to transcend the limitations of physical existence.

As you vibrate with the energy of unconditional love, thinking and doing slow down. You are content just to be present. Being present is enough, because in that presence is the love energy of the entire universe! It holds you and rocks you like a mother. It enters you and vibrates in your body. You feel warmth and tingling all over.

The healing power of love does not belong to any religion. It is not Christian, or Jewish, or Buddhist or Hindu. It is not exclusive or protective of itself. It spontaneously opens to bless, surround and inspire any human being who is ready to give it and receive it.

Your willingness to feel this energy of unconditional love in and around you will transform your life and the lives of the people you know. It will speed up the vibration of your life and at the same time slow down your mental activity so that you feel bliss you have never felt before.

It will be as if you are riding in a cocoon of positive energy. Soon you will no longer feel that you can support or participate in the negative fear-based patterns that you encounter. You won't want to judge or complain, blame or shame. You will find yourself turning off the TV and the computer, spending time walking in the forest or by a stream.

You will do what resonates with the energy of pure love and drop what doesn't. There will be no force or sacrifice in this. What no longer serves you will simply drop away as you more deeply attune to and vibrate with the truth of who you are.

Do not be afraid of any of this. Nothing will be taken away from you that you are not ready to release. This process goes forward only with your permission and your willingness. When you cease to be willing, it simply stops.

Divine Mother does not force you to love and be loved. She merely offers you the opportunity. She invites you to be present and accept the gift of Her love.

Once you have received this gift, it will vibrate in your body and in your consciousness, expanding outward to embrace your life and everyone in it. All that you do or say will be done with this energy and contained gently within it.

As you receive, so will you give. The reactive cycle of fear will be replaced by the creative cycle of love.

If these words resonate with you, draw close now so that the next phase of this work can move forward through you. May the blessing of One God, One World, One Presence rest within you and around you.

The Time to Wake up is Now

Today, you are called to drink the waters of the Holy Spirit. Today, you are invited into the great communion of hearts. Do not turn away this opportunity. It has come to you for a reason.

Take up this mantle and wrap it around you. Let the God of Love come into your heart. The sacred marriage is at hand and you are the bride. It does not matter if you are a man or a woman.

The energy of the One Transparent Being takes your hand and enters your body. Now you are filled with light. Now, the fire of Spirit baptizes you from within. Its flame burns in your heart like the burning bush of Moses. The tree of life burns and glows, but it is not consumed. Its warmth radiates out from your heart. Its subtle energy emanates outward from your hands.

Your mind is filled with illumination and peace beyond words. Past and future fall away. There is the ecstasy of Now, fully revealed.

You are the One who has come forth from the chrysalis. You are reborn into life as Spirit. Your arms and your legs carry the Living Word. Only truth can be spoken. Only love can be offered. You are the way, the truth and the light.

There is no unworthiness or lack in you

. The holy fire has burned all that away.

You are a servant of love. Your only purpose is to love. Therefore love yourself. Love your brother or sister.

Find no fault with self or other. Offer the blessing of love and acceptance to all.

Do not discriminate. Do not hold back. Do not question the call. Simply answer it in each moment.

The fire of divine love dwells within you and wraps you in its mantle. You are blessed. You are guided. You are protected. You are healed.

Go now and offer this healing and empowerment to others.

Who is Directing this Work?

The work is being guided by a kind of meta-consciousness that includes the energy Jesus embodied when he was here on this planet.

Christ consciousness is not limited in its expression to the historical Jesus nor is Buddha consciousness limited in its expression to the historical Gautama. The energy and con- sciousness of Christ or Buddha is available to all of us when we are ready to experience it. But we won't experience it until we "leave our nets," drop our fear-based patterns along with the guilt and shame that hold them in place.

We must say goodbye to our old limited life in order to enter the new life. For most of us, one door must close for another one to open. This cannot happen through force. The ego must not be ripped away. It must be ever so gently surrendered.

When we know it does not satisfy, that it does not bring lasting peace, we simply open our hearts to something deeper and wider.

To be in Christ Consciousness means to embody the energy of unconditional love and acceptance. To awaken to your Buddha nature means to move beyond duality consciousness into the oneness. Both are experiences of non-separation.

For thousands of years, religions have divided us. Now it is time to move beyond these divisions. All spiritual paths lead to God. One is not better than another. All can be celebrated and respected.

The meta-consciousness that transmits this energy to us is beyond dogmas and denominations. It is pure love, pure devotion. When we experience this, we simply drop out of duality consciousness.

It isn't hard. When your vibration is speeded up, the old ideas and modes of perception simply fall away. You are in the new energy, the new vibration, the new experience.

You are in the world but not of the world. This is a palpable reality. All of you who join with us in this work will experience this.

So, we ask, are you ready? Are you ready to let love take charge of your life? Are you ready for the new paradigm energies that will help you to build a world of equality and acceptance between brothers and sisters and bring a lasting peace to planet Earth?

Remember, the word must become flesh. And it is not going to happen through someone else. It is going to happen through you.

Societal and Planetary Transformation

Once you activate or rekindle the divine love energy in your heart, you will be guided to join with others to create the new paradigm houses of healing that will embody this energy at the community and planetary level. This will result in the creation of new schools, new types of work including those that are more collaborative, new hospitals, prisons, even government agencies.

The energy of unconditional love will go everywhere that is needed and bring healing and transformation with it. You don't have to make any of this happen. It will happen through you.

The idea of "making things happen" through focusing the mind, repeating affirmations, or engaging in rituals of magic or mind control is contrary to the Spirit of this work.

The divine love energy is your friend and your guide. It works with you and through you. As you learn to trust it, you simply turn over the direction of your life to it. You get out of the way and let it happen through you.

This is the new paradigm quality of the energy. It will result in a whole different type of creativity on planet earth.

This energy comes in at the nick of time, so to speak. By re-establishing the connection with the divine, it helps the human come back into alignment with planetary needs and to step into his/her stewardship role in protecting and nurturing Earth rather than in exploiting it. The real ecological watershed happens through a shift in consciousness. The new consciousness creates new realities.

The Nature of this Work You are Called to

Simply stated, you are being asked to be the instrument of love in a time of fear. Each one of you is part of the great constellation of love givers. You are coming together now to speed up the collective awakening of human consciousness on planet Earth. You are not the ones who will actually do this. However, the process will go through you. Your surrender to the energy of unconditional love in your body, your mind and your heart makes this possible.

Who is the Healing Facilitator?

The healing facilitator is one who has decided not to live for herself alone. She is committed to her own healing to be sure. She has made it a priority. But she is also ready to share the fruits of her journey with others.

She is not greedy or selfish. She is not competitive with her brothers and sisters on the path. When fear comes up, she recognizes it and realigns with the Divine love energy.

The new paradigm teachers and healing facilitators model the teaching. They embody love and acceptance. They are collaborative, cooperative, open, and strive to see the best in others.

They do not desire to fix or to save others. Instead they empower others to heal from within and to step into the fullness of who they are.

They know that when we heal we do not heal alone and they are committed to building a healing community for themselves and others. Because they have learned to get out of the way, this work of healing and transformation can be entrusted to them.

What your Role Is

You wear many hats and play many roles, for you are agents of healing and transformation on many levels. You facilitate healing by transmitting and awakening the energy of unconditional love. You counsel and teach using the concepts and spiritual practices in *The Laws of Love* and *The Power of Love* books. You minister to, guide, and inspire others. Your role is multifaceted. You serve the awakening of unconditional love and divine wisdom in the human family.

You are teachers of love, but you teach in many ways. You teach with words and without words. You teach with loving and healing touch. You teach by being silent and listening.

You are a bringer of love to yourself and others. You are the presence of love, the energy of love in expression, the power of love in action.

None of this is personal. It is impersonal. You are an instrument, a channel, a vehicle, a vessel that contains and transmits the energy of love and acceptance. You do your work with trust in the energy and in yourself. You know that your work is sacred and brings love to all with whom you work.

You work with individuals and with groups. You answer the call as you hear it. You serve. You celebrate. You show up where and when you are needed.

The Sufi's have a simple word for this extraordinary being who shows up when he or she is needed. They call it the Friend. You are the Friend. You are an equal brother or sister bringing love to yourself and others. You are a bringer of love, the living presence and embodiment of love in your consciousness and in your community.

Wherever you go, love goes with you. That is what you must remember. That is the essence.

We bow to the presence as it unfolds in each of you. It lives in you and fills you up till you are overflowing with it. And you live and rest in it, knowing that all of your needs will be met in the appropriate time and place.

The more you trust the process, the more it gives to you. And the more you receive, the more you have to share with others.

This is the economy of love. It is the kingdom of God come to earth. It is a great blessing.

One Love, One Heart

We remind you that what can establish in one heart can establish in many. First, you feel it in your consciousness and your physical body. Then you feel it in your group and in your community. Then you feel it in the community of nations, races, and religions.

The key to all of this is your heart. That is where all of this begins. When you truly accept love for yourself, you also accept it for all.

The Conductor

You are a conductor in the same way that a copper wire is a conductor of electricity. It enables electrical energy to move from the positive to the negative pole.

Those who are in the full consciousness of their divinity are the positive pole. There is not just one of us. That is why we say that we are a "we," yet the meaning of this "we" goes beyond anything that you can imagine.

Now, if you understand non-dual teaching, you know that the positive pole is contained in the negative one as a potential. It is dormant, sleeping, unrealized, but it is there nonetheless.

When the conductor touches you, the higher energies that are dormant in you are awakened. First he touches your crown, and then he touches your feet, creating an energy that flows downward through the chakras from heaven to earth. When this energy is fully grounded, he touches your heart. There the positive and negative poles are harmonized and you begin to vibrate with the energy, becoming fully charged, fully empowered.

In the Hindu tradition, it is common for the Guru to give Shaktipat to the student who is ready to awaken and become a container for the energy. Shaktipat is the fire of the Holy Spirit.

It is not so much that we receive this fire energy, as that the flame that is dormant in us is ignited and raised up in our body, our heart, and our mind. The inner current is stirred into motion. Once activated, the current moves between the crown and feet, centering in the heart, where most people experience it as a transmission of pure, unconditional love.

This pure love energy is the key to all awakening. When the

divine love energy is fully activated in the heart, the recipient is born again in love.

This spiritual rebirth comes after we have gone through the dark night of the soul. It comes after we have realized that our ego structure with its fears, demands and expectations cannot bring us peace or happiness. That is when we hit bottom and call out for help. That is when the universe hears our cry for help and the conductor is sent to us.

The conductor asks us one simple question: Are you willing to put the old fear-driven ways aside?" If the answer is "Yes," then the conductor can help us connect with the new, higher frequency energies.

In time, there will be many conductors, many instruments of the divine helping people to connect with their Source. And perhaps then it will seem that the instruments begin to play together, to love together, to join together in the great work. It is then that the symphony of equality and justice can be played in every city on the planet.

How the Fire in the Heart Spreads to Illuminate the World

Each one of you who vibrates to these words is a conductor of this energy to some degree. Sharing it with others is a way of deepening your connection to Source, so do not keep this energy to yourself. Give it gladly and freely. Be the expression of love in your life.

Don't stay in your box. Let go of the mental and emotional limits that keep you trapped in a lifestyle that no longer supports your growth and self-actualization. Leave your nets. Claim your freedom.

Know that you are not on this journey alone. Reach out to your family and heal the old wounds. Reach out to your brothers and sisters and create a safe place where all can be loved and accepted. Create sacred affinity spaces where people can confess and release their pain. Build spiritual families that support each other.

Step into your power and express your talents and gifts. Be creative. Assume your role as a teacher, a role model, and a leader. Inspire others to live to their full potential. Work with others in your community to build the new paradigm houses of healing where wounds are healed and forgiven.

Individuate. Detach from all outer authority and follow the guidance of the indwelling Spirit. Go where you are guided to go. Speak the words that you are given. Become completely present and authentic.

Then you will be a master. Having answered the call in good faith, you will be given the strength of heart and the tools that you need to fulfill your purpose here on earth.

This is what it means to be a light worker. It requires that you radically connect with your Essence/Source and nurture the spark within you so that it becomes a steady fire. Then your light intensifies and becomes visible. You become a beacon and others are drawn to you.

Each of you must enter the door of the heart and become who you most truly are. Then all that separates you from others will drop away. The ego will stand aside, bowing to the Presence of Love.

You will embody the Presence. You will be the door that opens, bringing others into the circle of Love.

Playing Your Part

Please understand. You are not asked to do more than you can. You are simply asked to play your part, to do what has been given to you now.

Every time you take a step, the next step will follow. You don't need to know what the third or the fourth step will be. Indeed, knowing that would just get in the way.

We are moving into a different consciousness. It is not driven by worry or fear. It is filled with the presence of love. It makes it possible for us to be here right now.

This is the consciousness spoken of in the Sermon on the Mount and you are all the lilies of the field. You are bathed in sunlight and sweet rain. Your needs are spontaneously met without struggle or hardship.

That is because you trust. You live in the present moment and know that it is always enough.

Abundance happens in this consciousness. This is where two fishes miraculously feed thousands and the water is made into wine.

Miracles are the fruit of unity consciousness. They cannot be created by our egos, no matter how hard they try. If you are trying to manifest money or cars or boats or whatever, you are universes away from the true meaning of abundance.

The true meaning of abundance is that there is enough here

for everybody. Poverty is unnecessary when the wealth already present is shared by all.

In the new paradigm reality, selfishness will be replaced by compassion and then both poverty and riches will disappear. Each person on the planet will have enough and know in his or her heart that having enough is far better than having less or more than s/he needs.

What is the Next Step?

The next step is to be yourself fully and completely. Drop your mask. Stop living the way others want you to live. Be true to yourself. You can never be true to others by betraying yourself.

Heed this call to come home to your True Self. Do not delay, hesitate or procrastinate any further. You are to step into your life work and be fully empowered within one year from the date you are reading these words.

Reach out to others and build your spiritual family. Meet with them weekly without fail. Establish a sacred space and bring the divine love energy into it. Invite all to come into the circle of grace.

Become the conductor in your community. Empower others so that they too explode in the fire of unconditional love.

There cannot be too many conductors. When there are enough conductors in one area, the work will automatically propagate and spread to other areas.

We are asking you to tell everyone about this work who has ears to hear it. Do not keep it a secret. Do not be ashamed of it or try to hide it. Let everyone know what your experience is.

Witnessing is not done with words alone. It is done through being present with others and sharing the energy. Practice the presence. Be the love that you are in every encounter.

Share openly what is valuable to you. If the words in this book speak to your heart, share them others. Start a study group or a book discussion group. Open the dialog with other brothers and sisters.

If your network is large, share this work with everyone in it. Don't accept limits. Let everyone know, but do not be attached to who responds. Your job is to get the word out, not to cajole, manipulate or preach.

Just show up and be willing to do what is asked from you in the moment. The words you need to say will be given to you. The energy will work through you. Without knowing how it happens, people's hearts will be touched. You will see.

The Guidance of the Masters

Today, you have access to all teachers in all traditions and to that energy that goes beyond teachers and traditions. You can directly experience the presence of unconditional love as energy, as warmth, as a vibration that lets you know that you are connected to the divine, to the heart of the universe, to the heartbeat of creation itself.

When you feel the energy, you know. There is no mistaking it. Therefore, the energy is an insistent reminder that you are not alone and that you have access to all the love and all of the truth in the universe. And so, having access to this, you cannot be limited. You can no longer be small. You can no longer be held back by fear, for you are already larger than any fear that you experience.

You have in the body an energy that goes beyond the body. In many respects it goes beyond the mind. To enter into the non-physical, non-conceptual dimension requires a connection to this energy. The energy takes you beyond words or concepts and beyond the limitation of physical form. It takes you into an expanded Reality beyond anything that you have known, although some of you have experienced glimpses of it in your time here.

Because of your connection to the divine love energy, your capacity to love yourself and to love others is now greater than at any other time in your life. What once seemed like a dim possibility is a present actuality. It is within your grasp. It is possible at this time for you to step into your creative fullness. It is possible for you to do things you only dreamed of, for help is here.

The energetic connection will support you in becoming all that you are. This potential for self-actualization and fulfillment is available now.

Rejoice. For this is the most extraordinary blessing. Only when you live in the energy moment to moment do you begin to appreciate the power and completion that comes through It.

To be the Christ, to be the Buddha, to be the Awakened One is to manifest fully not only the Self, but the All. All the great wisdom traditions and all of their master teachers express through you in this moment as One Love and One Truth.

We are entering a time in which all who are involved in this work will walk through the door that is opened to them here and become the door for others. That is the meaning of this time.

That is the significance of the availability of the divine love energy to all who are ready to claim it and live it and be it. As this divine energy is embodied in the physical, it begins to inform and shape the decisions that are made on the planet. For as consciousness changes, its creations necessarily change.

What we are talking about is simply the end of selfishness and greed on planet Earth. But this is not obtained through some moral agenda, as some would have it. The end of selfishness and greed is obtained through a shifting of consciousness from an I-centered to a We-centered consciousness, from a conditional love for others to a love without conditions.

That is the nature of the transformation that has begun on the planet and all of you are part of it. Each one of you is asked to lay down that which separates you from your brother and sister. It is no longer functional and, to the extent that you hold onto feelings and thoughts of separation, you will experience great difficulty and struggle in your life, for it is time that these thoughts and feelings are transcended.

Transcendence can happen swiftly if you are willing to shift into the higher frequency energies that are available to you now. Each one of you is giving birth to a new Self, an expanded Self filled with divine wisdom and love so that you can do God's work here.

This is a very exciting time, a time when you will experience extraordinary fulfillment. The presence of love will unfold in your life. It asks only your willingness to allow it to express through you.

You are the Bringer of Love

The time for hiding our love or withholding it from others is over. This is a time in which we must speak and express all of our love. In one way or another, through a smile, a pat on the back, a few encouraging words, we are asked to give the love to others that has been given to us.

The gift of love has not been given to us so that we could keep it for ourselves. It has been given to us so that we could live in it and with it and extend it to everyone in our experience.

When you align with the gift, you become Christ. You become Buddha. You become the Friend to all whom you meet.

The White Light

When you know that the Source is within you, your light body is clear, radiant, vibrant. There are no disturbances that block your light.

This pure, white light is a reflection of an inner certainty. You cannot "put this light around you," as many try to do.

The white light is present when you are in connection with your Source. It is the effect or by-product of that connection.

The words "See and know that I am God" represent the consciousness of your light body. When you see through and from your light body, you see and know the God in others, regardless of whether they see it or know it about themselves.

The white light is often portrayed as a kind of halo around spiritual beings. This is not just some artist's conception. The halo does in fact illumine those who rest in unity consciousness.

It is a full-bodied luminosity that any one who is sensitive can see. The light body is the expression of wholeness, completion, and connection to Source. When one is in one's light body, one needs nothing. One is completely Self-sufficient.

That is what the God-Self is. It is an individualized expression of the Abundant Whole.

Gathering the Seeds

You are seed gatherers, not seed sowers, for the seeds have already been sown.

The seeds that are close to the tree will be sheltered by the tree. They will be easily found and cared for. But those that fall far from the tree must be found and nurtured or they will not be able to sink their roots in the ground and grow into saplings.

Gather these seeds one by one. Remind them of their origin. Reconnect them with the sheltering tree of the spiritual community. And then take them back home and plant them in the ground.

Empower them to grow and build community where they are so that the little saplings can mature and become great sheltering trees. The work of love is a profound work. You are here to inspire others by example. By giving your love and sheltering others with your compassion and encouragement, you help your brothers and sisters step into their divine purpose.

As they awaken, they gladly reach out to help others. That is the nature of love when it takes root within consciousness. It is profoundly generous. It does not withhold itself from anyone.

The tree is awesome in its beauty. When it puts forth its leaves in the spring it becomes a home for all kinds of creatures. It is strong and splendid. It is a witness to abundance and grace.

The tree gives of itself and it keeps giving. In the autumn its leaves turn many-colored and fall from the branches. The tree is beautiful in its surrender. It goes willingly into the unknown. It dies and is reborn every year.

So are the teachers of this way. They die and are reborn many times, and each death is a purification leading to a deeper surrender. As the ego steps aside, the work flowers as never before.

Every spring is more magnificent than the year before. For the greater the surrender, the greater the capacity to bring the message of love and to be its embodiment in this world.

PART TWO
Our Divine Parents

4

Divine Mother

This is the secret, dear ones.
You cannot come to the Father
except through the Mother.

Return to the Feminine

In order to accomplish the great work of planetary healing that we are called to do together, we must re-connect to our Essence and to the Great Mother who gives birth to all life. This is a bigger challenge then many may expect, because human consciousness has been dominated for thousands of years by the male, outward energies and the patriarchal cultures they have created on planet Earth.

The male energies have fueled an outward exploration that has resulted in the conquest of all continents and countries on our planet. Tribal and indigenous cultures have been eradicated or displaced by these aggressive, and often violent energies. Traditional peoples have suffered greatly under the occupation of soldiers seeking fame and fortune. Peaceful villages where people lived in harmony and interdependence with nature have been plundered. The countryside has been decimated. Mountains have been excavated, rivers dammed up or re-routed. Women have been raped, children have been murdered and men have been sold into slavery.

This is the unfortunate legacy left by western culture run amuck. In the name of God and Country, human beings have brutalized each other. And this same aggressive, exploitive energy is alive today in our consciousness and our actions. We cannot afford to allow it to dominate our world. We must reign in its destructive forces and bring them clearly into our awareness. We must expose the wound behind the anger, the pain behind the attack. Only then will the reactive machine—driven by our collective unworthiness—stop its machinations, for it will run out of fuel.

Meanwhile, we must turn our own consciousness inward to connect with the great Mother and her nurturing energies. We must learn to find peace in our hearts and minds. We must learn that we are worthy of love and so is everyone else. Until we know this firmly and securely, all our creations will be driven by fear.

We are not repudiating the masculine principle. We will come back to it in time. But first we must connect to Mother's love. Then and then only will our actions be beneficial to ourselves and to others.

The world that we are being asked to build together cannot be created out of fear. It must be built with love.

In order to do that, we must return to the feminine principle and learn to embody it. We must surrender to Divine Mother and allow Her to teach us.

Communing with Mother

Every day Mother asks us to connect with Her unconditional love for us in our hearts. She asks us to wrap the gentle mantle of Her acceptance around us. She asks us to feel the warmth of Her embrace in every cell of our bodies.

This is the core practice in this work. We are asked to feel Mother's love when we get up in the morning and to remember it throughout the day. Whenever we feel anxious or unworthy, whenever fear, or doubt or anger comes up during the day, we are to remember Mother's love and give it to ourselves. We are to bathe ourselves in the fragrance and the vibration of Her love.

Her love is the foundation of our existence. For it is only when we are connected to this Source or Essence of our Being that we can live a spirit-rich life, a life that embodies the energy of unconditional love.

Before beginning this work, many of us do not have an awareness of, or a connection with the Great Mother. That is not surprising. She lives behind the scenes. She does not call attention to Herself. The Taoists call her the Gateway to the Mysteries. In Her dark, impenetrable, void is the origin of the Tao itself, or the Great Way of all beings.

Every individual being has its origin in the Great Being. All form has its origin in formlessness. From the dark womb of the Mother, the myriad things are brought into existence.

It is hard to talk about the Mother, for Hers is the primordial darkness from which the Father arises. Hers is the Infinite Kingdom before "Let there be Light."

Until Father comes on the scene, there is no differentiation, no up or down, no male or female. The Great Mother is the primal Unity. She contains all the opposites. Duality comes from her. But prior to duality, prior to separation, there is only Her.

She is the subtle essence we all take for granted. When we think about God, we usually think about God the Father. For it is His voice that we hear when guidance comes.

Yet Mother is prior to that voice. She is the silence in which the voice is heard.

Many people complain that they cannot hear God's voice. But that is because they have not yet entered the deep, fathomless cave of the Mother. Only when they enter that place and abide there, can the voice be heard.

This is the secret, dear ones. You cannot come to the Father except through the Mother. This is what Jesus was trying to tell us.

You must get quiet and learn to listen. You must become profoundly patient and receptive. You must cultivate acceptance of yourself and others. You must sink into the heart. For that is where Mother lives: in your heart of hearts. That is the manger. That is the secret place where the infant Christ lies swaddled and protected by Her love. That is the incubation chamber.

Do you think it was only Jesus that needed the incubation experience? How can that be? Mother's womb was not just for him. It was and is for all of us.

The Invitation of Divine Mother

The most important news of the day is not to be found in all of the trials and tribulations reported in the newspaper or on the television news. Nor is it to be found in the dramas that we play out in our personal lives every day. It is not to be found in the pain and misery we perceive within us or outside of us.

The most important news is that there is something that is right with you and me and with the world we live in. There is something in us that is whole and complete. It doesn't need to be redeemed or fixed. It does not need to be changed or revised. It is absolutely okay just the way it is. Nothing is lacking in it.

That is the news that Divine Mother brings to us today.

Throughout all of human history, that has always been Her message to us. "In this very moment," Mother tells us, "you are completely worthy of love and acceptance."

There are no hoops that we need to jump through to qualify. There are no tests to pass or missions to accomplish. Indeed, we need do nothing to be worthy of Mother's love. It is given to us unconditionally now and for all time.

Mother's love is not connected to what we "do" or "do not do." It is ours simply because we are here. Just by being present we can receive and embody all of Her love.

Unfortunately, most of us do not take the time to "just be." We don't take time to breathe and center and go within to connect with Mother's unconditional love for us. That is why the first Spiritual Practice asks us to do this sincerely every day.

Without connecting to love, we forget our origin. We get drawn out into the drama of life and live in reaction to it.

Jesus asked us to live in the world but not to be of the world. He knew that we have our priorities upside down. We are all running around looking for fulfillment in the world, but it is a useless journey. The world cannot give us what we want.

Buddha told us the same thing. That is why he asked us to cultivate non-attachment.

All authentic forms of spirituality ask us to abandon the search for love and security outside of ourselves. They tell us that the only true security is within. It can be found only in our direct connection with our Source.

So we need to go to Mother and ask Her: "Please show me how to love myself without conditions. Please show me how to accept myself in this radical and profound way."

And Mother will help us to get quiet and feel Her presence. She will teach us to hold the space of safety for ourselves so that we can know at the deepest level that we are worthy of love.

The Practice of Acceptance

Mother's way is the practice of Acceptance. She asks us to accept ourselves as we are. She asks us to accept others as they are. She asks us to accept life as it is in this moment.

We can do this practice only in the present moment. We cannot love yesterday or tomorrow. We can love only what is before us right now.

In order to connect with Mother's energy, we need to practice acceptance in each moment. When we are practicing, we are experiencing Her love.

When we forget to practice, we begin to judge, find fault,

condemn, or criticize. We compare ourselves to others. We expect things to be different from the way things are.

That is the beginning of our suffering, because things are not going to be different. They are going to be however they are. We cannot change what is. The attempt to do so creates misery all around us.

We cannot change what is. We can change only what we think about it, the way that we perceive it, or the way that we expect it to be.

All of us have ways of thinking that distort the true meaning of our experience as it unfolds. We all have judgments, criticisms, and opinions and all of these interfere with our practice of Acceptance. We need to keep reminding ourselves that "all of my judgments, interpretations, pictures, expectations, etc. are illusions." We need to keep telling ourselves that "what I think about this doesn't matter. It is irrelevant."

Our job is to accept and work with what is, not to resist it or try to change it. So we need to see our resistance as it arises. We need to see our attachments and let them go. We need to see our expectations and drop them. We need to keep bringing ourselves back to our simple, pure practice of accepting life as it unfolds, moment to moment.

"Not Fixing" is Mother's motto. She keeps reminding us that things are okay the way they are. They don't need to be changed or fixed. People may come to us with problems, but as soon as we try to fix their problems we are going to make them worse. So we need to stop trying to fix others. We need to let them be as they are.

You see, Mother knows that most problems are "problems of perception." In other words, most problems are subjective.

There is a problem because you perceive a problem, because you are judging or finding fault. In other words, the problem is not out there in the world. It is in your consciousness.

So if you recognize this, you can make a shift within your consciousness. You can see where the discomfort is and correct it. You can shift from judging to accepting.

The only time that doesn't work is when you make yourself wrong for judging and start to beat yourself up for doing it. That creates another level of suffering. So before you can shift out of judgment, you have to forgive your judgments.

In the end, you have to return to Mother's love. That means you have to come back into that state of consciousness in which you know that you are okay just the way you are. You can't do that as long as you are beating yourself up, just as you can't do it when you are judging someone else.

A related and helpful practice of Mother's is "Do no harm." In the Hindu religion it is called Ahimsa or Harmlessness. Gandhi was a great role model for this practice.

In approaching others, we say to ourselves "Even when I cannot love, even when I cannot accept, even when I cannot bless, I must do no harm in thought, word, or deed." We hold others harmless when we refrain from judging them, criticizing them, telling lies or gossiping about them. By refraining from such thoughts and actions, we give others the benefit of the doubt. We place them in God's hands.

The practice of Acceptance is a profound, life-long practice. It is the way that we work with the Divine Mother energy and embody it in our lives.

Mother Wounds

Those who have Mother wounds have difficulty accepting themselves and others. They don't feel worthy of love. They don't know how to nurture themselves or other people. To function in life, they often build a wall around their hearts and don't easily let anyone in. They have doubts and fears like anyone else, but they quickly stuff them. They are afraid to feel anything. They don't do well with intimacy.

There are two types of mother wounds. One comes from an absent mother or from insufficient mothering. The other comes from an over-bearing mother or from too much mothering.

People who received insufficient mothering don't feel emotionally supported. They are hungry for love and acceptance and often become involved in co-dependent relationships with substitute mothers in the attempt to experience the mothering they did not experience growing up. They are needy and often expect too much from their relationships. As a result, their relationships often end in disappointment and bring up old feelings of abandonment. Yet, even disappointment in love does not prevent them from desperately seeking approval and support from others. That is because they are afraid to stand alone. They experience intense loneliness and do not know how to find the inner strength to affirm themselves and their own experience.

People with this type of Mother wound need to learn to give themselves the nurturing they have been unable to find from their mothers and mother substitutes. They need to learn to go within and hold the space for themselves. They need to cultivate love and acceptance of self, moment to moment.

On the other hand, people who receive too much mothering often feel smothered or controlled by the mother's love. The mother often views them as an extension of herself and does not provide healthy boundaries for the child. The child may grow up feeling inappropriately responsible for the mother's happiness. This is a heavy burden to carry.

People who have this version of the mother wound have difficulty cutting the umbilical cord to mother. Even as adults, they are profoundly influenced if not emotionally controlled by their mothers. These folks need to cut the psychic umbilical cord to their mothers. They need to establish healthy boundaries.

If they do not cut this psychic cord, they will not individuate. They will not learn to be independent and self-supporting. They will not be able to receive the Father energy.

There is still one more pattern of behavior that is typical for someone with a mother wound. This behavior may stem from either too much or too little mothering. In this pattern, there is a forced cutting of the cord early in the child's life. This may happen because the mother dies or because she is abusive and the child must disconnect. In either case, the child cuts off all feeling. S/he detaches from the Mother and becomes independent early in life. Wearing a plate of armor over her heart, s/he does not believe that s/he needs anyone. S/he becomes determined to live without love or intimacy.

In yet another version of this wound, the child goes to war with the overbearing mother, fighting for her emotional life, pushing the mother away. Yet s/he never disconnects totally. So the war continues long into adult life.

Often a person with a significant mother wound does not have children. However, if s/he does, s/he may push her children away and force them to become independent prematurely. S/he won't be able to deal with their dependency on her. Perhaps s/he will hire a nanny or leave the child with others who can do the mothering work. Or perhaps s/he will abandon her children, just as s/he was abandoned as a child.

The adult child can't help but pass on some version of her mother wound to her children. S/he may become just like her mother, or s/he may go to the other extreme in an attempt to parent differently from her mother. However, if s/he has not done her emotional healing work, this attempt inevitably fails.

Like it or not, without doing our work, we pass the wound on. Unless we commit to healing our mother wound, we will project our pain onto others. If we have not had healthy mothering, it is unlikely that we will be good mothers. We just don't know how to do it.

Many wounded mothers abuse their children, push them away or even abandon them. Chances are, these moms are not aware of their wounds. Their behavior is reactive and unconscious. They do not see or feel the pain that they cause their children, because they never allowed themselves to feel their own pain.

They feel guilty about how they have treated their children, but they cannot access the guilt. It is buried deeply.

Bringing all of this up to the surface can be a scary proposition. The wounded heart would rather not go there. We don't want to face our guilt, because it is just the tip of the iceberg. Once we begin to admit our guilt and feel the pain that we have caused others, we begin to see the root of all that pain. We begin to feel the fear, the abandonment, the criticism or even the abuse that we experienced at the hands of our own mothers.

Yet if we don't have the courage to take the healing journey through our guilt and our pain, we will continue to sit on a keg of emotional dynamite. Sooner or later, someone with just the right kind of mother wound will come into our lives, and strike the match. Like it or not, our deepest wounds are bound to be triggered. Everyone heals, sooner or later.

We can save ourselves a lot of time and suffering if we have the courage to speak our pain and share it with others. But this is not easy for the person who has repressed her trauma and buried her pain. She hurts, but she keeps her secret well. S/he walks through life with an iron mask that says "I'm fine. Leave me alone. I don't need anything from you."

Of course, that isn't true. S/he needs a lot, but s/he won't admit her neediness. S/he will not reach out or let others in. S/he is cranky and difficult around others. S/he rejects their overtures of friendship or affection. S/he pushes love and intimacy away.

So others learn to give her a wide berth. And so s/he is abandoned yet again. However, this is a small and familiar pain. S/he would rather push potential partners away than open her heart to another human being and risk paying the ultimate price. On some level, s/he knows s/he has already paid that price and could not stand to do so again.

Such a person is walking around with a great, black psychic whole in the belly, for that is where the umbilical cord was ripped away. That is where the wound is and will remain until s/he has the courage to face it, until s/he has the courage to ask for the love and acceptance s/he so desperately needs.

Of course, to get what s/he needs, the mask must come down. S/he must allow herself to be vulnerable and needy. S/he must open her heart and let others come in.

Both men and women have these and other versions of the mother wound. They all boil down to an inability to receive love.

Of course, if we can't receive love, we can't give it either. If there is a mother wound, chances are there is a father wound too. Often, when our relationship with the mother is difficult, we overcompensate and embrace the father energy with far too much zeal. Or we become like our mothers and attract a partner like our father who is weak, distant, or emotionally unavailable.

Too little of one parent often means too much of the other. Either way, we lose the balance required in the psyche.

All people with the mother wound must understand their pattern and work to heal it. Unless our relationship to the feminine principle is healed, our relationships with our mothers, daughters or female partners cannot be healthy. Moreover, we will not stand in the right relationship with our Source. We will not feel connected to the Essence of our Being, for that is what Divine Mother is.

All of us with mother wounds need to learn to let love in. We need to learn how to receive the unconditional love and acceptance of Divine Mother. We need to learn to give Mother's love to ourselves.

Divine Mother's Ministry

Mother's work is all about creating safety, support and nurturing for her children. And we are all her children, even those of us in adult bodies.

The family is the social mechanism created to embody Mother's energy. It is through the home and the hearth energies that children are protected and given a safe place to grow up.

Today, home and hearth have little nurturing energy. We live in a mobile society. People live active lives and do not even meet around the dinner table.

In most homes, both parents work, often long hours. The feminine, nurturing presence that holds us, listens to us, and quietly supports us is absent.

We live in a time when the majority of families are wounded, if not broken. Children do not feel safe and supported. And, if we tell the truth, parents don't feel safe and supported either.

What used to be created automatically with the blessing, if not the dictum, of the community, now requires our conscious attention if it is to thrive. We must bring the heart energy back into the home. We must find a way to create safety there for our children and for ourselves.

If we cannot create a safe space in our own family, we need to create new spiritual families where we can receive unconditional love, nurturing and support. That is what the Affinity Group* process enables us to do. That is why it is an essential practice in carrying out Mother's work.

---

* For more information about *Affinity Groups*, please see the book *Living in the Heart* by Paul Ferrini

Today, we all need Spiritual families—small groups of loving and supportive people gathering weekly—to facilitate the heart–centered communion with our Essence and that of others. That is how we experience our Oneness with the Divine and with each other.

Mother asks us to create spiritual families not just amongst our friends and those who share our race, religion or economic group. She asks us to reach out beyond those boundaries to all human beings: black and white, women and men, rich and poor, young and old. She encourages us to create a place—indeed many places—where the stranger and the outcast, the sick and the weary, the hungry and the homeless can take refuge.

To create such an extraordinary place of safety, we must first experience it. We can do that by joining an Affinity Group and working with the guidelines. The guidelines challenge us to look at our judgments with compassion. They invite us to hold ourselves and others harmless. They encourage us to accept everyone and everything just as it is in the moment.

Gradually, we begin to feel the ecstasy of living in and from our hearts. We know this is what we want to experience, not just once per week, but every day of our life. So we venture forth from the safety of the nest. We start creating an affinity consciousness and an affinity community wherever there is a need for safety and support in our world.

Having been nurtured and empowered by Divine Mother, we go forth from Her primordial womb, as God the Father did, to create. We say, "Let there be light." We offer our gifts to the world.

Passing the Torch

Our preparation is important. We can't rush the mastery process. The egg needs the nurturing warmth of the mother hen, so that the chick can grow to maturity. Impatience is not helpful. If we rush the birthing process, it will abort.

So we need to breathe, be patient, and know that the chick will be born exactly when he or she is ready, and not a minute sooner. The *Mastery* student must learn to trust the process. He or she must abide with the Mother until the protective shell of the ego starts to crack open.

Meanwhile, Divine Father bides His time. He knows that you cannot be a student forever. The time will come for you to step forward. He has worked with Mother long enough to know that he cannot rush Her process. So He waits patiently.

When you have cultivated self-love patiently and truly, an energy begins to build in you that requires expression. You cannot hold that energy back. It must break through the shell. The chick must be born. The gift must be offered. It is no longer an option to hide your light under a bushel any more than it is an option for the chick to crawl back into the shell once it has cracked open. There is something final, irrevocable, and extraordinary about the act of birth.

Doubts and fears move aside and the power of love manifests. The bright bird of Spirit is born and is ready to serve.

This is the moment that Divine Father has been waiting for. This is the time when the torch is passed from Mother to Father. The time for nurturing has come to an end. The time for empowerment has arrived.

5

Divine Father

Because of Father, we leave the safety of the nest.
Because of Father we learn to trust our gift
and give it to the world.

The First Flight

Whereas Mother keeps the newborn birds in the safety of the nest, Father pushes the fledgling birds out of the nest so that they can test their wings. Father teaches them to fly and to hunt.

Whereas Mother is all about love and acceptance, Father is about works and service. Mother is about being; Father is about doing. Mother is about receiving; Father is about giving.

Because of Father, we leave the safety of the nest and begin to earn our wings. Because of Father, we learn to trust our gift and give it to the world.

You cannot live a life of Spirit without learning how to give your gift to the world. Your creativity is not optional. It is necessary. Without it, the world is cheated and so are you.

In the nest, you learn your worthiness, faith and trust. In the air you learn your proficiency, self-confidence, and the ability to take risks.

Father helps you develop your skills and abilities. He helps you refine your talents and express them. He is your biggest cheerleader. He eggs you on. He tells you that you can do it.

Those who have father wounds have difficulty being in the world. They have trouble making a living. They don't learn skills or develop their talents. They are afraid to express themselves for fear of criticism. They are afraid to take risks for fear of failure.

They keep trying to climb back into the womb. They keep on making excuses for why they "can't do it." And if those excuses are accepted—if no Father steps forward to block their retreat and insist that they move forward, fears and all—they will not achieve mastery.

Divine Father's Mission

Mother cannot accomplish the work of redemption on planet Earth without the Father energy. She nurtures us and prepares us to do Father's work and then she gives us over to Him.

Father's work is much maligned and misunderstood. For it is not about fixing. It is not about converting, cajoling, or proselytizing. After all, His work is an extension of Mother's.

To understand His work, you have to see what would happen without Him. Without Father, the bird would not leave the nest. The great leaders, healers and teachers of the world would stay closeted in their Affinity Group. They would remain in seclusion in a futile attempt to hold onto their bliss. But it would not work.

In the end, the energy would ramp down. Because the love was not being extended, it would not renew. The more they suckled at Mother's familiar breast, the more Her milk would dry up.

Why? Because love is meant to be extended. Because Mother is not the only mother who must give birth and nurture her young. All of us must become mothers. She is the Great Mother but her true greatness is known through us. What we receive from Her we must learn to give to each other.

And who do you think is our Teacher? Who do you think Mother calls in to wake us up from our milk-imbibing trance?

That's right. She brings the only one in who knows how to kick our butts and motivate us to get out of the nest. She brings in the only one who is not afraid to pry our lips off the teat and onto a pacifier.

Perhaps that's why Divine Father has never been too popular. Yet He is the only one who can teach us how to give the love that we have received.

The Extension of Love

Although it is hard for us in the beginning to admit that all we want is love and acceptance, in time it becomes self-evident. We look forward to attending our weekly Affinity Group, because we know that our spiritual family is going to hold us with great love and gentleness. We know that the group is helping us reconnect to our Source. It is teaching us experientially to hold ourselves and others with acceptance and with love.

When the ten weeks are over and its time for the Affinity Group to end, it's hard for us to say goodbye. We want to stay in that group forever. We find ourselves thinking that the group itself is the Source.

We forget that when we first attended the group, no one knew each other. We were all skeptical about each other and about the process. Coming to the group was a big risk for us. We knew that the Process would ask us to stretch, to go beyond our ego agenda. We were a little nervous, uncomfortable. We wondered how we would ever be able to open our hearts and entrust our deepest fears and dreams to this motley group of strangers.

How things change!

Ten weeks later, we are afraid to leave the group. We don't know how we can live without the intimacy, the unconditional love and support. We don't think it will be possible to trust another group the way we have come to trust this one.

So we talk to others in the group. We try to convince the others that we should keep the group going.

That's when Divine Father shows up wearing his storm boots. "Enough of that kind of talk," He says. "Time to move on. Pack your bags. These folks are not special. The process teaches you to open your heart. Once your heart is open, anyone can come in, even the stranger."

Of course, we know that He is right. Still, we are perturbed at His interruption. We think He could have had better manners. He could have been more gentle and compassionate.

Divine Father always gets plenty of flack, because nobody likes being rousted from the nest. Nobody likes having his butt kicked out of the monastery.

"Why can't He be sensitive like Divine Mother?" we ask accusingly. We forget that She was the one who sent Him. We forget that He is the one who has answered Her call to help us build the houses of healing for our time.

Divine Father helps us to learn a very hard lesson. He helps us to realize that we lose love when we stop giving it.

As soon as we make love special and refuse to share it, it shrivels up. Only skin and bones remain. To stay fresh, vital, invigorating, love must be shared constantly.

We must continue to stretch and to take risks. We must go where we are needed, even if it seems a little strange or scary.

Divine Father asks us to be creative and proactive. His energy is outward. He asks us not to reach back, but to move forward. He is the one who tells us "If the process works in White Plains or Hyde Park, it will work in Zaire and Ethiopia." He won't rest until the houses of healing have been created all over the globe.

Father knows that for Mother's work to be complete and for her vision to be fulfilled, there is a lot of work to do. That is why He is always egging us on and waving us forward.

The Reign of Joy

Father's work is joyful because we always enjoy what we do in a heartfelt way. *Following our bliss* is one of the essential ingredients of Father's work. *Giving our gift* is the other. We need to develop our talents and skills and offer them with enthusiasm.

No other work is possible for one who has been reborn like the Phoenix in the Spiritual fire. The first half of life may have involved struggle and sacrifice, but the second half of life is about mastery and self-actualization.

Those who have truly been born again in Spirit can no longer live life in survival mode. They have already done that. They are called to greater things.

Each knows in her heart of hearts that she must do what she came here to do. The Advent has arrived. It is time to take the journey. It is time to express her greatest passion and contribute her greatest skills. It time for her to shine and be a light unto others.

The first half of life is preparation for the spiritual journey. The second half is the journey itself.

That is why Jesus called to Simon Peter "leave your nets." The time had come for the journey to be taken.

To take the journey, one leaves the past behind. One leaves behind the struggles of the world. One releases the entanglements of worldly life for a life of freedom and surrender to God.

Simon did not say to Jesus: "But Master how can I live without fishing. Who will feed my family?"

He said, "Yes, I am coming now." His was a higher calling. He was not looking for security in the world. He was looking to hear the truth and to become it.

As long as we have something we are afraid to lose, we will hold back. We will hang on to the past. Only when we have nothing to lose or we are willing to lose everything, can life unfold for us without effort. Jesus called his disciples to live on grace. He did not offer them a salary with benefits.

"Consider the lilies of the field, how they live," he said to them. "They toil not, yet are they live abundantly."

Countless students have told me over the years what their passion is. Yet in the next sentence they tell me why they cannot "follow their bliss." They have many excuses. But the bottom line is always this: "I don't trust enough. I'm not willing to take the risk. I'm afraid that if I let go of my security, I'll become a drifter or a bag lady."

That is why Jesus did not bother to call their names. Why bother? They weren't ready to answer the call. The disciples, on the other hand, were ready to risk everything. That is why Jesus called to them.

Each of us needs to ask the question "Am I ready to answer the call when it comes? Am I ready to let go of the past and be born again into a new life? Am I willing to let go of my need for security and live a life filled with grace?"

These are not easy questions to answer. Let us not pretend that they are. But let me suggest something to you. It does not matter how many times you have said "No." Sooner or later you will say, "Yes, I am ready. I have experienced the gifts of this world. The gift I seek now cannot be given to me by the world."

The master told us "Lest you die and be reborn, you cannot enter the Kingdom of Heaven." Of course, he was speaking in metaphors. He wasn't asking you to take your own life. He was asking you to "die" to the old life. He was asking you to let go of the anxieties and worries of daily existence. He was asking you to let go of attachments and entanglements. "Let all this fall away," he was suggesting, "and then you can live on light and on truth."

The Kingdom of Heaven is not in the world. It is in your

heart. You cannot enter it until your heart is engaged. You cannot enter if you aren't willing to follow your bliss. You can't enter it as long as you are still making excuses.

The creative spirit within us is the God light. It must shine its light no matter what the risk. A great voice must be heard. A great painter must have canvas and paints. Imagine if Caruso had never learned to sing or Van Gogh had never found a paint brush. That would have been tragic both for them and for us.

Like them, we are here to actualize our full potential. We must not settle for less. We must not sell ourselves short.

The challenges of the world cannot be met unless each one of us contributes our best. Everyone's gift is needed.

Don't worry if your gift looks different from that of others. If you are making a necklace, you have to have the string and the jewels. Don't denigrate your gift if you bring the string. Without it the necklace cannot be created.

Some have gifts that are flashy and attract great numbers of people. Others have more modest gifts that nurture and inspire a few. Both are necessary.

Some people are great at building armies. Some are good at leading them. Others are good in battle, in supplying the troops or in ministering to the injured or the dying. An army needs all of these people.

God's army needs your gift and mine. All gifts are equally important.

Father Wounds

People who have difficulty manifesting their life-work have father wounds. Perhaps the father was absent or unavailable while they were growing up. As a result, they did not have someone to help them develop the skills, the self-confidence and the discipline necessary to be effective in life.

Such children often lack drive and motivation. They are not encouraged to leave the nest and become independent, self-reliant people. They are coddled, overprotected and ultimately held back from discovering their gifts and expressing them.

Often the absent Father syndrome goes hand in hand with the overbearing mother syndrome. Lack of fathering often means too much mothering. When that is the case, the child tries to live through the mother and please her. His desire for her love and approval prevents him from being himself. Often, he carries this pattern into adulthood, marrying a dominant woman just like his mother. He lets her make the decisions for him and never learns to take responsibility for his own life.

He is like the boy who never grows up. He cannot live without "mommy." Even when one mommy dies, he keeps the pattern alive by finding another woman to take charge of his life.

Men and women with this type of father wound are the victims of low expectations. They never had to work and overcome obstacles to succeed. They were not challenged by life. Someone always supported them and protected them.

While low expectations of the child can be hard on both boys and girls, it is particularly difficult for boys. They don't receive the role modeling they need to become men. As a result, they have trouble putting bread on the table. They don't easily find their gifts and, even when they do, they lack the confidence to express them.

Men and women with this wound don't know that they can survive on their own and they are afraid to try. Instead, they play it safe. They stay in the protective womb of their relationship, because it is too scary to leave that security behind.

They feel trapped, yet they aren't. The door is open and they could walk out of the prison any time. But they won't do it. To be sure, they will bitch and moan. They will tell everyone how unhappy they are. But they won't do anything about it.

They will not take charge of their lives. They will not make their own choices and be responsible for them. No matter how much they complain, they will not engage their inner resources. They will not awaken their joy or commit to expressing their creativity.

They do not follow their bliss, not because they are incapable of doing it, but because they have never been forced to leave the nest. Is it any wonder that they don't know how to fly?

These people desperately need male role models who can teach them to believe in themselves. They need father figures to help pry them off the all-too-available-teat and send them out into the world to make a living. They need tough love.

At some point, they may have to come to terms with the fact that mommy's love for them wasn't exactly healthy. They might need to get in touch with some anger around that and they might need to use that anger to push away from the dominant women in their lives.

For unless they do that, they will become casualties of the mother's overbearing love. Their growth will be arrested. They will remain children forever.

They also may need to get in touch with their anger at their fathers for not showing up in their lives. They might need to see how that anger has pushed away the love and affection of other men in their lives. This too is part of the wound.

In the past it was easy to be with women. They didn't have to work to get mommy's love. In a sense it was too easy to get.

The question they must ask is not, therefore, "Did I receive mommy's love?" but "at what price did I receive it?" If the cost of receiving mommy's overbearing love was losing daddy's love, then that was and is too high a price to pay.

People with this version of the father wound must reclaim their relationship with their fathers and the other men in their lives. They must reach out and go the extra mile.

Although they want connection with their children, these fathers are afraid of intimacy. They also feel guilty for having abandoned their children, so it is easier for them to stay away than it is to ask for connection.

So those with this daddy wound must reach out. They must learn to say to the daddy, "Your love matters. I need your love. I need to be connected to you." And they may also have to say "I used to be angry at you for staying away, but now I have forgiven you. I am not angry at you any more. Please come back into my life."

Of course, the risk one takes in reaching out is that daddy won't respond. He won't take us into his arms. He may even tell us to go away and leave him alone.

But taking the risk is essential. It is a milestone in our lives. And even if the daddy of origin doesn't respond, we must open ourselves to the connection with other males who can mentor us and guide us. For until we reclaim our relationship to the masculine principle within ourselves, we will never be able to experience Mother's unconditional love for us.

For mommy and the other dominant women in our lives have loved us conditionally. They have loved the attention and the power we gave to them. But they have not loved us. Indeed, they have never known us, because we have never been allowed to be ourselves or express who we are. Healing our overbearing mommy/distant daddy wound requires that we get distance from the dominant females in our lives and reach out toward the men who can gently push us out from the nest and teach us to trust our wings.

This, of course, is only one of the two major father wounds. The other wound is caused by the Overbearing Father.

Those with this opposite type of father wound usually have controlling fathers who try to run their lives. They grow up doing what daddy wants them to do. They do sports because daddy wants them to do sports. They go to law school or medical school because daddy wants them to go. They never have the chance to find out who they are or discover their own priorities because they are living "daddy's vision" of their lives.

Daddy's control over them is not just emotional. It may also be financial. Perhaps daddy isn't going to support an interest, a career goal, or even a marriage that doesn't meet his approval. He is gong to support only what he thinks is good for his son or daughter.

Those with this father wound tend to do one of two things.

They either submit to daddy's control and let him run their life, or they rebel and thumb their noses at daddy, often doing everything they can to offend or disappoint him, just to make the point that he is not in charge of their lives.

Either of these extremes can be disconcerting. If the child submits to daddy's control, he lives an inauthentic life. He goes to a school that he hates. He does a job that he despises. He marries someone passive who allows him to be the same kind of daddy to his children that his father was to him. As a result, his children grow up hating him just as he hates his father. Not a happy scenario, to say the least.

Moreover, one of these days his shadow is going to rise up and rip his mask away. In his attempt to deal with his demons while maintaining the façade of his life, he may become an alcoholic or a pill pusher. Or he may be caught in the wrong place with his pants down or with his hand in the corporate cookie jar. But sooner or later, the façade will implode or be blown away. He will have a nervous breakdown. His life will fall apart.

The Spirit within him will no longer allow him to betray himself. He will be forced to come clean and tell the truth. He will have to tell his controlling father "Sorry, Dad, I tried to be the person you wanted me to be, but I couldn't do it. It wasn't me. Now I know, regardless of the price, I have to be myself."

He will empower himself from within. He will set himself free. If he chooses, on the other hand, to fight his father rather than submit to his father's control, he will alienate the father. He will lose his father's financial and emotional support. He will reject the authority figures in his life and may engage in danger-ous, self-destructive behaviors. Whether his life falls apart or he finds a way to make it work on his own, he may hold onto his anger toward the father. He may continue to push the father away, even when the father asks for his forgiveness and tries to make peace. His relationship to the male principle and to his own masculine energies remains wounded.

Whereas the healing of the first father wound requires standing up to the father, the healing of this second father wound requires forgiving the father. By accepting his father as he is, and understanding his father's limitations, he can reclaim the relationship with the father without betraying himself.

There are many more permutations of the father wound than we can list here. Let us remember, though, that both women and men have these father wounds. And if you are a woman with a father wound, you may have to read the above paragraphs over again, substituting "she" for the word "he."

Both women and men have healing to do with their fathers and the other men in their lives. They also have healing to do with Divine Father, especially if they grew up in a shamed-based, patriarchal religion where God is angry at His children and punishes them for their mistakes.

When our relationship with the Father is healthy, he encourages us, teaches us, motivates us, and cheers us on. Like a great coach, he gets the best out of us. He points out our mistakes with humor and compassion, without shaming us, so that we have the desire to correct them. So he gets steady improvement. He gets us to really believe in ourselves.

He knows when to get in our face and when to give us a pat on the back. He helps us understand the talent we have and how to maximize it. He also gets us to see our weaknesses so that we don't try to play selfishly or beyond our ability. He encourages all of us to work with what we have, to take the shot when it is open, and to pass the ball when it's not.

Like a skillful coach, Father tries not to set the bar too high or too low. For if he sets it too high, we will get discouraged. And if he sets it too low, we will not develop the full range of our talents.

Being a coach, and having a competitive nature, he knows that if he is going to err on one side it will probably be on the "high" side. That's why he is glad to have Divine Mother at his side. He knows She will always lower the bar when it is necessary. After all, our greatest successes are not won at any cost. They are won because we do our best and know that, win or lose, it will be good enough.

The Synergy of Mother and Father Energies

From Mother we understand that we are already lovable and that everything that we do is acceptable. We are enough. There is nothing lacking in us. And from Father we understand that we can always improve ourselves. We can always increase our skill and become more effective in our lives. From Mother we learn self-acceptance. From Father we learn self-actualization.

Both are important. When we internalize both the divine Mother and Father energies, we are motivated to give our love and to do our service, but we always know that whatever we achieve is acceptable, so we can be at peace in each moment.

Mother Teresa was not just the loving Mother taking care of

her children; she had strong Father energy. She would stop at nothing to reach her goal. She was a "make it happen" person. I have heard it said that even the Pope would shake in his boots when Mother Teresa came knocking on his door.

You couldn't say "No" to Mother Teresa. Her "Yes" was so strong it compelled you to participate. She was like a mighty river moving to the sea. No one was going to stop her from reaching her destination.

So, you see, Father energy is not just something boys have. It is something that both men and women need to be successful in the world.

When Jesus asked us to "be in the world" he wasn't asking us to hide our light or to become inconspicuous. He was asking us to witness, to serve love, to be the embodiment of the teaching. Being in the world means becoming a master, not being a "wimp." It means being a mover and a shaker, as Jesus was. After all, it wasn't a "wimp" who overturned the tables of the moneylenders.

Many see the soft side of Jesus. To be sure, he was gentle and compassionate. But he was also fierce. He was also a warrior for the truth and he was not afraid to stand up against hypocrisy and injustice wherever he encountered it.

So when Jesus asks us to "be in the world," we need to understand that he means that we are to be here in our strength. We are here to express our gifts fully and to empower others to do the same. He is asking us to use all of our skills and talents. He is asking us to step up to the plate with all of our resources.

But he is also asking us not to be attached to the outcome.

He is asking us to be at peace with whatever we are able to accomplish. He is asking us to give our very best and to know and have faith that it will be enough.

Jesus was an extraordinary blending of Mother and Father energies. He walked among us as a powerful teacher, yet he remained gentle and compassionate with all of his followers. He was a charismatic presence, yet he was not caught up in the drama around him.

Jesus did the work of Divine Mother. He was her loving emissary.

Yet he also served Divine Father. He had Zeus energy. He was fiery and uncompromising.

Avoiding Extremes

Father only accomplishes His mission by doing Mother's Will. That means that the ends and the means must be congruent. We can't talk about love and acceptance unless we model it.

The houses of healing need to be built with the Father energy. We need to get the tools out and start sawing and hammering. But at the same time, we must remember that we are building a holy place, a sanctuary, a place that will embody hope and love. So we must hammer and saw with love in our hearts. We must work joyfully.

There are two extremes that must be avoided in this work. One extreme involves too little Father energy. It expresses as the tendency to sit around and wait for God to show up and do the work for us when we are fully capable of doing it ourselves. We must remember that spoiled children with low expectations of themselves and others cannot build the house of God. Motivated, determined workers are needed, or the building will not be built, even in a million years.

The other extreme involves too much Father energy. This is the "make it happen" energy that forces the square pegs in the round holes. It pushes the river, drives people beyond their capacity, is always in a hurry and under pressure. It leads to hasty decisions that result in all kinds of problems and delays. When that type of energy manifests, there is a need to slow down, breathe, listen and tune in. We need to stand back from the job and look at it. We know from experience that haste makes waste, so we have to learn to be patient and let the project take the time it needs.

Mother and Father energy blend nicely when we know that we can't make anything happen, yet also realize that nothing happens by itself. We have to do our part. We have to be willing, proactive. We have to take risks, not foolish or reckless ones, but measured ones. And we have to be willing to slow the pace down when it becomes manic or stressful.

We need to listen for guidance and act on it. We need to see our mistakes and learn from them, knowing that we are living in a process that is unfolding with us. That is how the House of the Lord gets built . . . not perfectly, but with the grace that redresses error and brings acceptance of the little mistakes we all inevitably make.

We live in a time when we are facing many pressing challenges: global warming, pollution of the air, water and ground, terrorism, weapons of mass destruction, the rise of new infectious diseases for which we have no cure. All of us know that apathy and inertia on our part will result in a steady deterioration of the quality of our lives and may significantly endanger the lives of our children. How can any of us not know this?

Yet at the same time, we cannot allow ourselves to be motivated by fear to act in ways that are hasty or shortsighted. We need to connect with Divine Mother's energy of love and acceptance, so that we meet the challenges before us with love and compassion.

It is with this blend of Mother and Father energies that we will be able to build the houses of healing for our time. We need to find this balance in our own consciousness if we want to create it in the world.

As the old patriarchal civilization crumbles around us, both matriarchy and patriarchy must be laid to rest. This is not a time for one extreme or the other. It is a time for balance.

Father and Mother dance together as equals now. Because of that we too can give birth to the dance of equality and justice on Planet Earth.

6

Divine Guidance

God has a way of knocking on the door to our hearts.

Opening the Dialog with God

God, being immanent and invisible, has only us to represent Her/Him. S/He cannot go forward into the world except through us. We are the arms and legs of the divine. We are Its witnesses.

It is the people of God who serve God's people. We are here to serve each other, to remind each other that we are worthy and lovable.

You might think that you are here to fix computers or make airplane parts or invest in the stock market, but that is not why you are here. You are here to serve, to awaken, to be the embodiment of love.

"But I am not religious. I don't even believe in God," you say.

It doesn't matter whether you believe in God or not. That doesn't change anything. The divine spark lives in every heart.

And one day, with or without warning, it ignites and becomes a bonfire. You can't ignore it. You can't pretend that you don't feel the heat.

God has a way of knocking on the door to our hearts.

We can't turn away or decline the invitation, because we are the one who wrote it. We said, "I am willing to serve. Please, God, just give me a chance."

"But I don't remember saying that," you maintain.

Well, you might not remember, but that doesn't mean that you didn't say those words. Not remembering truth doesn't make truth untrue. It just postpones your recognition of it.

Sooner or later, you will realize that you are here to serve and only your service means anything. Everything you have done in your life up until the time when you hear the call is just treading water. It doesn't amount to much.

"But I don't know how I am called. I don't know what I am being asked to do."

Then ask God "What would you have me do?" Ask and keep asking every day, in every situation. "What would you have me do here, Lord?"

Start asking and you will receive the guidance you request. God talks to everyone who is willing to listen. And God will talk to you right now, if you seek Her/Him with an open heart.

Opening up the dialog with God is essential if you are going to discover the divine plan for your life. So come to God with an open mind and an open heart. Come in surrender. Bow at God's feet and say, "I am here, Mother and Father. What would you have me do?"

Once you establish the dialog with the Divine Presence in

your heart, It will guide you and it will be up to you to follow that guidance. Of course, it won't always be easy. Don't be surprised if God asks you to stretch a little or to say or do something out of the ordinary. God always has many surprises.

In the beginning you may be tested because God wants to know that you are sincere and reliable. God wants to know if you are really listening and if you are willing to carry out the instructions you have been given.

I remember once giving a workshop somewhere in the Boston area and I could tell that one of the women in the audience was having a hard time with the material. As I noticed this, I heard an inner voice tell me "I want you to give that woman a refund!" I tried to ignore the voice, but at the break, as I was going downstairs to use the bathroom, this woman came right up to me and told me that the workshop was not what she had expected and asked if she could have her money back.

Because I had already received my instructions, I didn't have to think about it. I just looked at her and said "Sure. No problem."

You can argue with God and negotiate with Her/Him, but in the end you have to let God decide. S/He knows things that you are not privy to, at least for now.

The Servant of Love

Once you are in dialog with God, you stand in a whole different relationship to your life and to the world than you did before. You are in a partnership. You no longer meet life alone. You have a companion, a guide, a friend wherever you go.

Increasingly you learn to rely on God to give you the words to say and the places to go. You are willing to show up and be used as a mouthpiece, as an instrument of the Divine Will.

The surrender to God, however, is not surrender to an outer authority, but to an inner one. You surrender to your inmost heart, to your essence, to the Spirit within. That is who speaks with your voice, walks with your legs, and reaches out with your hands.

God is the indwelling presence, the vibrating energy that lives in your heart center and effortlessly extends to others. Now, when you open your arms to hug other human beings, they are able to receive a direct transmission of that energy into their hearts, if they are open. The same energy will pour through your hands when you reach out to touch someone with love and acceptance.

Your whole body is filled up with this divine love energy. You embody it. Your cup is filled to the brim and it overflows. Energy literally pours through your hands and feet. Healings happen around you. People feel empowered, accepted and loved.

That is how you know that God, or the Presence of Love, is with you. And all you do is show up. You don't do the healing. You don't even know what words will be said through you. You simply show up as the instrument and all of this is done through you.

When people try to make you special, when they try to worship you or put you up on a pedestal, you say what Jesus said: "Without God I can do nothing. All that comes through me comes from the Divine Being. I can take no credit."

And you encourage others to give as they have received. You tell them "Open to receive God's Love for you and extend it to others. For you cannot keep it if you do not give it away."

God's love is a gift. The energy and power of love do not

come from us, but through us. We are the fountain that receives and transmits the living waters. But S/He is the water. It is the Presence of Love Itself that heals, forgives, encourages and uplifts.

Once the divine energy is fully embodied, we become as Jesus was—the anointed one, the Christ. We become love's body, love's arms and legs, love's mouthpiece.

The promise that Jesus made to us—that we would do as he did and more—becomes fulfilled. We no longer need to stand under the fountain receiving the love and blessing of our teacher, because we become the fountain itself.

The light of Christ shines through us. The Buddha nature is awakened in us. The Tao lives in our hearts and vibrates in our words.

This is what it means to awaken, to light up, to be filled to overflowing with the energy of love. That is when our service becomes a constant blessing to all whom we meet. For nothing remains of our old ego structure. All that is swallowed up in the purifying fire. And only what is of love, only what is of God remains. We are truly reborn in Spirit, not as a man or a woman, but as the Servant of Love.

Self Care and the Care of Others

One does not become a Christ or a Buddha without first becoming a responsible human being.

I have said many times that the love of God flows through our love for ourselves. And it also flows through our love for our brothers and sisters.

Our first assignment on the spiritual path is to learn to love ourselves without conditions. In order to do that we must accept ourselves, warts and all. We must learn to see our inner perfection and let go of our need for outer perfection. We must accept the mistakes that we have made and learn from them. We must come to terms with the ways in which we have been careless or hurtful to ourselves or to others. We must practice forgiveness on a daily basis.

Acceptance of self cannot happen until we have cried our tears, expressed our anger, and overcome our shame. It cannot happen until we really know that we are worthy of love. It is a simple concept, but it takes many years of consistent and energetic practice to come to a broad and compassionate acceptance of ourselves.

Our second assignment on the spiritual path is to learn to love others without conditions. And here too acceptance is the key. Unless we are willing to accept others as they are, all we will be able to offer them is conditional love.

Accepting others means that we stop trying to fix them, change them, heal them or redeem them. We know that they are fine just the way they are. We see their inner perfection and release the need for them to be outwardly perfect or to fit our pictures of the way we think that they should be.

Just as self-acceptance means that we have to encounter, forgive and ultimately bless our own shadow side, so acceptance of others means that we have to witness with compassion the painful and wounded places in others. We must be willing to forgive their mistakes and trespasses, just as we have forgiven our own.

Being a Christ or a Buddha requires a human apprenticeship. We don't give birth to our spiritual perfection without learning to accept and forgive our human imperfection.

Self-care and the care of others are the pathway to spiritual mastery. Along the way, we will be asked to chop wood and carry water, and clean a few latrines. The path is not a glamorous one. We are asked to do whatever needs to be done. Because a Buddha or a Christ doesn't throw a tantrum or refuse to show up when he doesn't get the karma yoga assignment he was expecting. He just smiles and takes up the bowl and the brush.

The purification process is meant to uproot every ounce of impatience, selfishness, pride, and stubbornness that exists in our consciousness. Wherever the obstacles to love are in our psyche, they will be found and dissolved. If we resist, the process will take longer.

We move through the purification phase in direct proportion to our willingness to heal from our wounds. The more willing we are to do our emotional healing work, the more quickly we move into the higher states of consciousness that bring grace and clarity into our lives.

Impatience and Denial of our Wounds

Reading spiritual books does not necessarily help us wake up and take responsibility for our healing process. Many people reading spiritual books are unwilling to look at their fear, their anger, or their shame. They don't want to see their impatience or their greed. They don't want to make a moral inventory, confess their sins and ask for forgiveness. They want to skip over that.

So they intellectualize. They live in their heads and attempt to bypass the emotional body. They read spiritual books and often teach them. They go to workshops or they give them. They learn to talk the talk convincingly. But their lives never light up. They stay in the same self-centered patterns. The same pain keeps recycling through their consciousness and experience.

That's because bypassing the emotional body does not work. It is an exercise in denial. In the end, life will bring them a wake up call they cannot ignore. Then, they will drop their mask, feel their pain and ask for help.

The irony of the healing process is that the more you avoid or deny your pain, the more it is prolonged. So, if you really want the fastest and most direct path to enlightenment, you have to feel your pain and walk hand in hand with your fear. It is a rather steep path up the mountain, but there are places to rest along the way, many of them with wonderful vistas.

On the other hand, if you are lazy or impatient, there are plenty of people who will sell you a ticket to heaven. They will tell you that their rocket ship can get you there in less than five minutes and that the ride is super smooth. Of course, you have to buy a one-way ticket, but that won't deter you if you are determined to take the easy way out.

I know of jihadists in every religion who purchased that kind of ticket, including the guys who flew the planes into the World Trade Center, thinking they would be having dinner with the Prophet Muhammad that very evening. Others drank the Kool Aid in Guyana or attended Appelwhite's slumber party.

Well, friends, there is nothing we can do about that. The rocket ship to heaven has always been a best seller, even without much marketing. It seems to speak to people's aversion to the real emotional healing work that precipitates spiritual growth.

Perhaps now, after the media has exposed enough cult murders and swamis caught with their hands in the cookie jar, we are beginning to wise up. The sugar daddy doesn't deliver. In fact, he doesn't even know how to fly the plane.

At long last, we are beginning to realize that we get only as much as we put into our spiritual practice. Moreover, our spiritual work cannot be done by others. It is our responsibility, our commitment. And it requires daily discipline.

There are many cul de sacs for the new age spiritual aspirants who try to get to God without walking on the ground. In the old days, they wouldn't have made it more than a week in the monastery. But now you don't have to go into the monastery for forty years to learn the great spiritual teachings. You just have to click on your mouse and go to the Internet.

With the Truth so readily available it is easy to miss, especially if we try to pop it like a pill. Then, when we don't get instantaneous results, we're off looking for the next great miracle drug.

Of course I'm not suggesting that miracles are impossible. I'm just saying that nothing much is going to happen on the quest for the divine until we learn to show up and do our work. Reading the words and internalizing them are two totally different things. If they weren't, we wouldn't need this *Course in Spiritual Mastery.*

The Mastery Process

This *Course* asks you not just to understand the concepts intellectually. It asks you do daily and weekly spiritual practice that will help you to open your heart to love's presence. It asks you to embody the teaching.

When we first presented the *Course in Mastery* to you, we told you it was a ten-week program. Those of you who were sincere in your practice quickly realized that the first ten weeks were only going to scratch the surface. You knew you were going to have to go through the Ten Laws and the Ten Practices again or maybe even several times to really understand and internalize them

Indeed, many of you realized that you could spend six months to a year just working on the first five spiritual laws and practices. Not only that, but you required support from the program and from other students to stay committed to your practice. With a year or more of steady, patient practice, you could begin to see concrete results in your life. You could see that you were growing in self-love and self-confidence and beginning to realize your potential as a unique, creative human being.

And so, after a year in the Mastery program, you are ready to take on the challenges of sharing your light with others. You are getting in touch with the gifts you have to offer and the house of healing you are here to serve. You feel ready—at least in some small but significant way—to step out of your comfort zone, to step into your community and be the light and the truth you have been reading about.

That is when your ministry begins: when you accept your gift and begin to offer it. That is when Divine Father stands with you as you take the first few courageous steps into fulfilling your life purpose.

In this way, you embody and transmit the presence of Love, as others masters have done before you. You become "the way, the truth, and the life" because the Spirit of God goes with you.

This is your ordination on the path. You are placed in service by the power of love itself.

If you aren't ready to step forward yet, it's okay. You just need a longer incubation period. Give yourself over to Divine Mother's embrace and be held in the nurturing womb of Her love. She will strengthen you and prepare you for the role you have volunteered to play in the shift of human consciousness from fear to love.

It is only a matter of time before you will be ready to serve and Divine Father takes your hand.

Soon, there will be only two types of people remaining on the planet: those who are connecting to love in preparation for service and those who are actively serving.

So welcome, dear one. We have saved you a place at the table. Your presence is needed. Your unique gifts are required. Your participation in the drama of at-one-ment is essential.

PART THREE
Answering the Call

7
The Call of the Children

Mother's Children are calling out.
Have you not heard their cries in the night?
Have you not heard them knocking at your door?

Taking Responsibility for our Creations

If human consciousness is to be sustained on planet Earth, we will need to stop denying our responsibility for the conditions we have created around us. We will need to begin taking responsibility for the health of our bodies, our hearts and our minds, the health of our communities, and the health of the planet we live on.

We need to understand that it is up to us. We are the ones who will decide whether life as we know it will go forward or come to an end. We are in the times that T.S. Elliot spoke of when he said the world will end "not with a bang, but with a whimper."

This is a time of many tears for the human family and the other creatures on the planet. We humans have created incessantly without acknowledging our mistakes or correcting them.

That must come to an end. We must recognize now that we are responsible for everything that we think, feel, say and do.

Today, Right Thinking is not just an ideal that we aspire to. It is a logistical necessity. If we do not look carefully at our options and make the right decisions, we will be sealing our own fate.

Today, living a compassionate life can no longer be just a goal that we set. It must become a way of life, a daily practice. Today, we are called to practice forgiveness of self and others, to let go of grievances, and to stop projecting our anger or our shame onto others. Today, we are asked to take responsibility for healing our wounds. We are beseeched to turn our swords into ploughshares.

Today, we are called to cease speaking the language of separation, the language of denial, the language of attack. We are asked to speak only words of love and encouragement. If other words come out of our mouths, we must recognize and atone for them.

Today, we are called to act not only for our own good, but for the good of all beings. This means that every action must be scrutinized and put to the test. We must ask "Is this for my highest good? Is this for the highest good of others?" And if the answer is "No," we must pause and consider what manner of suffering we are about to create.

It used to be that we had plenty of time to make mistakes and learn from them. That is no longer true. We no longer have plenty of time.

I do not say this to be discouraging. It is important to be realistic about where we stand.

Yet we need to have faith, because things are not going to

remain in their present state of dysfunction. As we begin to live from the heart and be directed by the energy of unconditional love, the time-space continuum will begin to shift. Time will slow down. There will be more spaciousness in consciousness, along with the opportunity to reflect, to tune in, to engage our inner knowing. As a result, our thoughts, feelings, words and our actions will become more clear, focused and energized, and they will have greater impact on those around us.

As we live in accordance with the laws of love and continue our spiritual practices, we will begin to create in a harmonious and responsible manner. We will begin to build loving community around us. Where hearts and homes are broken, the seeds of hope and fellowship will be sown.

Wherever we go, we will create safe places where people can heal and be supported in their healing process. The work of collective transformation will go through us. Indeed, this is the work we are called to.

That means that wherever there is fear, hopelessness, or hostility around us, our loving presence is needed. We can no longer walk away and say "I don't want to be bothered."

We need to be bothered by all forms of inequality, injustice, dis-ease or suffering. We need to stand up for ourselves and for our fellow human beings with love and with faith. We cannot be pushed back or pushed away. We need to stand in love.

The justice that will come to planet Earth is not justice for one at the expense of another. It is justice for all. In the world we are creating, we are all equals. No one is special. No one is more entitled to the resources of life than another.

Divine Mother wants to feed and house all of her children.

She wants to bind up their wounds and nurse them back to health. She wants to create safety and support for all of the children of Planet Earth.

Hearing the Cries of the Children

Today we live in a topsy turvey world. As women have entered the workforce, focusing on the external challenges of making a living, running companies, competing for jobs, and climbing the career ladder, the energy of the hearth has faded. Children are being mothered by television, computers and video games. They are being prematurely and pervasively exposed to gratuitous sex and violence. The magic of childhood—the joy and the playfulness—has been sacrificed to the grim realities of the street, where gangster rap blares at dangerous decibels, drugs are universally available, and automatic weapons rule.

The child growing up today must find his way in a world in which human beings hi-jack airplanes and fly them into buildings, where no one is safe on a bus or train, on a bridge or in a tunnel, a world in which the worst of human creations —weapons of mass destruction—can be delivered in a suitcase or in a letter in the mailbox.

Humans have found new ways not only to kiss, but to kill, not only to bless and encourage, but to torture and maim. And what stories are told on the news? What human "works" claim our attention? What "examples" do we publish in the paper or over the airwaves?

As we view the daily carnage—the beheadings and the explosion of body parts—even the most desensitized of us have difficulty finding faith and hope. How can we expect our children to cope? It is, my friends, too much to expect. For many kids, the damage has already been done.

Is it any wonder that many of our children have decided to tune out the insanity around them? Is it any wonder that many kids are unable to live without prescription drugs for ADD, depression, anxiety, and insomnia?

Parents too are overwhelmed. Perhaps that is why we have been far too willing to find a chemical band-aid to strap over our children's wounds and our own.

Now we know the band-aid just doesn't work. The treatment exacerbates the wound, creating a new generation of addicts and wards of the State.

We hoped that medication would help our kids be functional in school. Instead, it made them more dysfunctional. Many dropped out of school. Many could not find or keep a job. Many today are on public assistance. Many have severe depression or eating disorders.

Still others are suicidal, or homicidal. Some have been ostracized or humiliated by their peers. We have seen more than a few of them walk into school with automatic weapons and open fire on their teachers or their classmates. They think that dying like video-game heroes is better than living in a world where they don't seem to fit.

The world we have given our children is a world with little hope, a world of pipe bombs and metal detectors, a world where kids are forced to grow up way too soon, which means of course that they don't grow up at all. Their emotional development is arrested.

Far too many of our children are victims of PTSD. Each day they come home with battleground trauma. For that is what our schools have become: a place where some are wounded in the head and others in the heart. If you want to understand the severity of the trauma, ask them to tell you what they dream about at night.

It's time that we began to face the truth: Humpty Dumpty has fallen off the wall. We didn't hear the crash, but we can see the pieces scattered across the floor. And we know that we are the ones who will have to pick them up and try to put them together again.

It may be an impossible task. It won't be easy to get a generation of children off Ritalin and Prozac. But we need give it our best shot. We need to call in all of the king's horses and men and get busy.

Ironically, things often get worse before they get better. Drugs anesthetize the pain. When you take away the medication, the pain comes back and you have to deal with it. You have to ask "Why am I in pain?" You have to realize that there is wound there that needs to heal.

After all, pain is a wake-up call. If we don't hear it, we don't wake up. We don't heal.

Our children are in crisis and so are we. We need to find a way to recreate the safety and support of the family. The hearth has to be mended. Mother and father—or their equivalents—have to show up around the dinner table. The nurturing presence must return to the home.

New Schools for New Kids

Divine Mother's love is needed not just in our families, but also in our schools. They must become places where kids feel safe, supported, mentored and challenged to develop their talents and their gifts.

We have to face the grim reality. We do not have many authentic classrooms where real learning can happen. What we have is the shell, the façade. The building is there. The teachers are there. The students even show up day after day. But learning doesn't happen.

Here we are trying to teach math, English, history, physics, etc. when someone's best friend just overdosed or got ambushed by gang members. In this environment, it isn't easy to keep your mind on algebra or the rules of grammar.

Kids need survival skills and we haven't got the slightest idea how to teach them. They need counseling and information on birth control, STDs, substance abuse, etc. They need anger management, conflict resolution techniques. They need support groups, encounter groups, coaching, mentoring, role modeling. You name it. Most of them don't need a school. They need a halfway house or a therapeutic community. They need outward bound, boot camp and sensitivity training. But most of all they need attention: simple, unrehearsed, undiluted, human attention from people who care, people who will help them set realistic goals and work toward them.

Over 50 years ago, A.S. Neill created a school called Summerhill. It was the flagship of the free school movement where kids were given the power to make decisions over what they learned and how they learned it. At the time, it was an interesting experiment that was no doubt way ahead of its time.

Now, its time has come. Now, the level of alienation and disconnection is so profound among our young people that only the most patient and persistent adults will be able to get through to them. Only those adults who can sink through the mental haze into the emotional riverbed of their lives will be able to coax them back to work or the classroom.

Terra Firma is a long way away for most of them. Although they can do wonders with a mouse or a joystick, they are the least practical and the most ungrounded generation in human history. Yet they are the ones who will be at the helm of the ship when the storms come.

Are we going to write them off or help them step up to the plate? If we look deeply, we will see—in the depth of their collective heart—a genie waiting to be summoned.

They have not had their wake up call. They have not had a reason to live. They have not been told that they are needed, until now. And we must tell them, again and again.

"This is your world and lest you engage with it, grapple with its challenges, and learn to serve it, it will follow you into oblivion. You are the hope of Planet Earth. Do not sell yourselves or the planet short.

It is time to re-create the world as it was meant to be and you have signed up for the task. So wake up. Pay attention. Didn't you hear your name being called? Don't you see the sign on the back of the chair? It has your name on it!"

Crimes against Women and Children

The statistics tell us that one out of every three women has been or will be sexually abused at some time in her life. That means there is someone in your family, someone close to you who has been abused. It might be your mother, your sister, or your daughter. It is might be your wife. It is that pervasive.

The assault on women and the feminine spirit has happened throughout recorded history, but only now are we beginning to acknowledge it. Only now are we creating enough safety for women to come forward and get the help and the healing that they need to overcome their shame and self-loathing.

Only now are we beginning to understand the nature of abuse and why it happens. As a general rule, people treat others as they have been treated. That means that they do not abuse others unless they themselves have been abused.

For abuse to be ended, once and for all, the chain of healing must reach as far back as the original wound. Not only must the survivor heal and forgive herself, but the perpetrator must also heal, and so must the one who abused him. The anger must be expressed. The shame must be lifted.

All abuse is terrible, but sexual abuse is particularly damaging. For sex is designed to be an expression of love and a celebration of intimacy. It is meant to be a holy and hallowed act in which we experience the ecstasy of joining with another. But when a caress becomes a fist, when tenderness is replaced by brutality, heaven and earth cry out in protest. That which is meant to be given in surrender is taken by force. Is it any wonder that the survivor feels betrayed not just by the perpetrator, but by God Himself?

When we fully understand the trauma in our ourselves and our fellow human beings, we no longer wonder why it is hard for us to work, hard for us to love, hard for us to trust. And we realize that unless we take the time to heal our wounds, we will be the victims of our traumas for the rest of our lives. We will be the walking wounded, the ones who perpetually push love away because we are ever afraid that Jekyll will turn into Hyde, or that when we least expect it, the bottom will fall out of the barrel.

Denial just doesn't cut it any more. The conspiracy of silence must end. Such secrets cannot remain hidden. We must have the courage to speak, however scared we are, to let others know, however much our voice shakes when we open our mouths to tell the truth.

The crimes that have been committed against women must be spoken, investigated, and atoned for. Each woman who has been hurt deserves her day in court, her confrontation with her abuser. And each abuser needs to feel and confront his own wound. He needs to feel the pain he would deny and give instead to another.

The healing of the survivors/perpetrators of sexual abuse, physical abuse, ritual abuse is a major house of healing for our time. Few people want to take on the task of building this work, for it is not an easy one. Many facilitators are afraid of being triggered and having to deal with whole new layers of healing from their own wound. But somewhere, sometime soon, a champion will arise, and Spirit will work through him or her to create a safe-place for survivors to heal.

Successful Houses of Healing

Many years ago my friend Elisabeth Kubler Ross was asked to teach a class on death and dying at the University of Chicago. When she did the research, she realized that death was not a subject people liked to talk about. The more she looked, the more she saw that we human beings were in denial of our mortality. To maintain the shell of denial around us, we sent our loved ones off to die in nursing homes or hospitals where we would not have to witness their guilt, their fear, their suffering unto death.

They were not the only ones who were short changed by our absence. We were cheated too. We were not able to experience our own fear, guilt or grief. Instead, we stuffed them.

It would take many years of new paradigm work in the field for us to realize that being afraid of death and protecting ourselves from its sights and smells leads not to a richer life, but to a kind of living death. In denying death, we deny ourselves the opportunity to live with heart and soul. We deny ourselves the compassion we are here to learn how to give, not just to others, but to ourselves as well.

Elisabeth took the band-aid off the festering wound. She forced us to look at the wound and to tend to it. The result was the construction of one of the greatest houses of healing of our time.

Today her ministry continues through many others who are devoted to helping people make their transition with love, support and dignity. Yet this is only one of many houses of healing that are necessary for our time.

If you look at the deepest place where you hurt, if you look at where you are angry or afraid, if you look at where you feel shame or great anxiety, you will see where the band-aid needs to be peeled back. You will see and know where you must allow yourself to experience the pain so that you can begin to heal from it.

That, my friends, is where your house of healing is. That is where you need to reach out for support and help from those who have similar wounds. Those who have experienced healing and self-forgiveness can help you experience them too, but you must take the time to hear their story, to be inspired and empowered by their example. And as you heal, you will understand that your continued progress depends on your willingness to reach back and help others heal too.

Dr. Bob and Bill W. demonstrated the power of a loving and supportive community in midwifing addicts into sobriety. The Twelve Steps of *Alcoholics Anonymous*, along with the foot soldiers who embodied the principles, gave birth to one of the great houses of healing of the twentieth century.

These are two examples of successful houses of healing. Many other equally compelling houses of healing must be built in the Twenty First century. And each one of us must be open to hearing the call and stepping forward to do our part.

If truth be told, there is not a single institution in our society that is not sick or in crisis. Alarm bells are going off everywhere.

The prisons are overcrowded. Dangerous criminals are being put on the street where they are nearly certain to commit new, violent crimes. Others are released from jail without having learned the skills to make an honest living. And a few are being put to death by lethal injection, even though their guilt is questionable and they have found a new ways to live that benefit others.

The health care system is in shambles. Millions of people are uninsured. Others are deeply in-debt trying to pay off hospital and doctor bills. Many medical treatments are questionable or cause worse symptoms than the ones they are supposed to cure. Insurance companies refuse to pay for wellness programs or natural healing approaches that could save them money and bring health care costs down. Drug companies bring drugs to market that they know are not safe. They refuse to develop low cost products that are effective when they can keep higher priced, but less effective drugs on the market.

We can no longer ignore these challenges. It is time that we hear the cries for help from human beings who are being exploited or treated cruelly by the institutions that purport to serve them. The old system is dying. It can't be propped up any more. We need to let it die and put our energy into developing a new vision for human life on planet Earth.

8

The Real Revelation

We will not be afraid to look at what we have done.
We will come to the Kingdom
with eyes wide open.

The End and the Beginning

The Book of Revelations is perhaps the most grim and gory scripture ever written. It is "Old Testament" in its flavor, telling the story of how God's wrath is visited on human beings who have not kept their covenant with Him. It is a fiery tale of mighty earthquakes, mountains sliding into the sea, and angels wielding thunderbolts. Even the heavens are angry. Stars fall into the earth and the sun and the moon go dark.

In Revelations, Jesus opens up the Book of Life and presides over the judgment of men and women. In this black tale, Jesus gets even for the crucifixion and all those who persecuted the early Christians get their due. John must have taken pleasure as he described the hellish torments suffered by those who did not accept Jesus as their savior.

Now I can understand John's anger and his desire to right the wrongs of the past, but my take on God and on Jesus is very different from the one portrayed in Revelations. I don't believe that Jesus would take pleasure in judging us. Indeed, I don't think he would judge us at all. Did he not teach us, "Judge not lest ye be judged?" Did he not forgive his executioners, beseeching God "Forgive them for they know not what they do."

No, I don't think Jesus wants to punish us for our wrongdoings. I don't think he is interested in being an instrument for the wrath of God. His testament is a testament of love and forgiveness, not a testament of judgment and punishment.

Revelations is one of those stories that presents the ego's version of its own punishment. Is it any wonder that it is gory and grim?

Yet there is a seed of hope even in this dark, dreary tale. For Revelations talks not only about the destruction of a human world that is out of step with God and with its own goodness; it also tells of the new world to come. In that world there will be a shining city and people will at long last live in peace. In the New Jerusalem, heaven descends to earth.

I appreciate that vision and the hope that it brings. But again, I have a very different take on all this.

I don't believe that either heaven or hell will descend to earth. Both, I suspect, are here and have been here for all of human history. And which one will prevail, I suspect, is not up to God, but to us.

If we were to ask God or Jesus which one they would wish upon us, I have no doubt what their answer would be.

No, I don't believe that the coming challenges for planet Earth are God's way of punishing us. I don't think we are being chastised for being bad. Indeed, I don't think that global warming, hurricanes, tornadoes, earthquakes, terrorism, weapons of mass destruction, disease, starvation, homelessness, or mass murder have anything to do with God.

To me these tempests have a human, not a divine origin, and we humans are simply experiencing the consequences of the choices that we have made. Our karma is up and it is time for us to deal with it.

But this also means that we have a choice right now. We can learn from the mistakes of the past and stop repeating our errors. We can learn to create responsibly and in harmony with the laws of love or we can continue to ignore the spiritual and physical laws that govern our experience. It is up to us.

In the next seven years, we will be making that choice. I assure you it is a profound one.

We are living in the times that Revelations talks about and yes, there is a process of purification going on. But what is happening now is not about punishment for our sins. It is about taking responsibility for our choices. That means all of the chips are not yet in. The jury is still out. The votes are still being counted. Sorry brother, John. In the end you might be right about where we end up, but you will not be right about how we got there.

The angel may come bringing the sword but s/he won't be the one to use it. In the end, when evaluating the cause of death, we will have to rule "Suicide. Death by his own hand."

However, while the jury is out, let us seize hold of brother John's vision of the New Jerusalem. It may not descend from the sky, but no matter. Even if heaven does not come to earth, earth can reach to heaven and embrace its laws. We can learn to be gentle with each other and to co-Create with God. We can build the kingdom of heaven right here on earth, stone by stone, brick by brick.

And frankly folks, that is what we are going to have to do. Because the old edifices cannot remain standing. We need new skins for the new wine, new buildings for the new vision.

T.S. Elliot told us "the end is where we start from." The New Jerusalem is muscled out of the debris and the dust. And dust, of course, returns to dust. Cycles begin and end. Civilizations rise and fall. No empire lasts forever.

Just as the seeds of death are present at birth, so the seeds of the new life are present at the moment of death. So let us not despair. The phoenix does not mourn the ashes scattered around him. He drinks them in. His breath is full of fire.

This is a time not only of endings, but of beginnings. Alpha and Omega are the circle of fire whirling around us and what dies now will soon be reborn. Even as we gaze at the funereal pyre, the bright bird of hope is taking shape in the flames.

In Hinduism, Shiva is considered the greatest of the three gods that form the triune godhead. To be sure, he can be tough, even ruthless. After, all, he is the destroyer.

Brahma is the one who gives, but Shiva comes to take away. He is the one who burns the crumbling building to the ground.

Yet without Shiva, Brahma has no room to create. The old must die for the new to be born. Shiva is merely preparing the way for that which is greater than anything that has come before.

Even Jesus told us that we would be baptized in the flames. He told us that he would come with a sword. But that sword is not the sword of judgment, as many think. It is the same sword that Shiva wields. It cuts away our attachments. It loosens the knot of our entanglements. It sets us free from our chains.

Shiva is the great liberator. From him, Brahma is given a new slate, a new canvas on which to paint. Without the release of the old, how can the new be born?

For Jesus, Heaven was not in the sky or in a life beyond this one. Heaven was right here and right now, but to see it and experience it, we had to take off our dark glasses. We had to let go of our judgments, our prejudices, our limited, selfish thinking. To find Heaven, we had to learn to change our minds and open our hearts.

Jesus was already living in Heaven right here on earth. He didn't have to die to get there. He did not have to be crucified. His body did not have to be sacrificed to reach the heavenly state. That was a fate not ordained by God, but by men of closed hearts and narrow minds.

God did not need Jesus to be crucified. We did.

God's hands are free of any stain. His mind is without guilt, for it was not He who pulled the trigger, hammered the nails, or let the blade of the guillotine fall.

We did. We are the ones who killed our brother.

It is time that we fessed up to the crime. It no longer works to blame anyone else. The time for scapegoats is over. We committed the crime. And we must atone for it.

In World War Two six million Jews were put to death. God did not kill them. We did.

Many humans are angry because God did not intervene and stop the carnage. But let us remember, God did not intervene for Jesus either.

God is powerless to stop man's inhumanity to man. Only we can stop it.

If God could stop it, he would stop it, don't you think? Why would God be sadistic or devoid of compassion? And if He were, how could we worship such a God?

No, I'm afraid none of this ads up. The old paradigm religion where God smites us from the sky or stands by while millions of people are slaughtered just doesn't cut it any more.

We aren't willing to worship a God like that!

No, God, if He exists at all, is a loving and compassionate God. He does not attack his people. He does not ask His son to die on the cross.

Unless, of course, His hands are tied. Unless—because He made us in His image, a creator like Himself—He left it up to us. Unless He gave us free will, and refuses, no matter how bad it gets, to take it away from us.

And that, I propose, is where we started this journey—eons ago—way back in the Garden of delights—and where we find ourselves today, in the post-Garden, post 9-11 world. And today, the terrorist, as well as you and I, has the same choice that Cain had when he looked at Able and felt envy and hatred well up in his heart.

This, if truth be told, is the only choice that we have ever had. All men and women who have come here have been given the same choice.

Even now as we teeter on the edge of oblivion, the same

choice lies before us, not just individually, but collectively. We are about to make that choice, once and for all time.

The Tears of the Mother

On the hill you can see where
the crosses once stood
and the centurions
crouched
counting the nails.

White puffy clouds blow in
like the white gowns
of the mothers
who listened in despair
to the screams of their sons.

But the sky is bright blue
and no one remembers
how the field
was once covered
in blood.

Yet right now in a different place
in a different time
another order is given:
the doors are broken down
and the soldiers enter.

This I am told
is the will of my country:

the children lying
face down in the hallway
the barrel of the gun
thrust into the belly
of the pregnant woman.

Later, on the news
as if in slow motion
you see the bus round the bend
but you do not hear
the screams.

They are swallowed up
in the sound of the explosion
as the roof comes off the bus,
glass shatters
and the windows implode.

This is not the only place
where the tears of the mothers
flow like a black river.
It is not the only place where crimes
have been committed.

Somewhere in the dark shadows
of the church
the boy's testicles are groped
and his lips forced down
onto the priest's penis.

Weeks later, hardly blushing
the priest denies
his involvement, lies
without feeling remorse
or guilt.

Cain does not want anyone
to know what he did to Abel.

Either way,
the sin must be hidden
the wound covered up.
The tears of the parents
are bought by the Bishop.

The leak is plugged,
the wound sealed up
in an uneasy cloud of silence.
You wouldn't want to say
anything bad

about your church
any more than you would want to say
anything bad about
your country
or someone in your family.

You wouldn't want to be put on the spot
or forced to testify
even if you saw it happen
with your own eyes.
You wouldn't want to admit

you had anything to do with it:
husband raping wife
brother abusing sister,
no witnesses to report
the crime,

no signs to explain
the loathing of self
or the loss of innocence.

Dear Jesus
in the name of freedom
a village destroyed,
women raped in front
of their children.

In the name of religion
people blown up
while eating in a restaurant,
sleeping in a hotel,
or going to work in a subway train.

Unless they meet
in the afterlife,
the bombers
will not see the faces
of their victims.

The generals will not see
the blood on the boots
of their soldiers.

The bishop will not see
the betrayal or the humiliation
in the altar boy's eyes.

But you, dear Lord
know all of this.
You know
your blood
is still on our hands.

9

The New Jerusalem

And God shall wipe away all tears from their eyes;
and there shall be no more death, neither sorrow, nor crying.
REVELATIONS 21:4

And so, my friends, the time has come to take spaceship Earth off automatic pilot. We know what happens if we don't.

We need to wake out of our stupor. Things will no longer take care of themselves. Actually, they have never been able to take care of themselves. It's just that we had a longer grace period before, so we didn't sweat the consequences of our inaction. We didn't have to deal with immediate, precipitous casualties. But now bodies are piling up all around us, just like they did after the Tsunami in Indonesia or after Hurricane Katrina hit New Orleans.

We are not used to seeing a whole city under water. It is a strange and disconcerting sight.

It is even stranger when we realize that meteorologists and engineers had predicted the event many years ago. Had we listened, the huge loss of life could have been avoided. But who listens when he thinks the danger is not imminent? Who wants to move a whole city or even a part of a city for the sake of something that might happen in 5 or 10 years?

We humans do not like to be inconvenienced. Government doesn't have the resources and we don't want to be uprooted even if we live in a dangerous place. It is not until the danger has materialized and the damage has been done that we are amenable to change and then, of course, it is too late.

So there you have it. We can anticipate some of the problems that we are going face and make choices now that will mitigate damage and minimize loss of life in the future, or we can wait and be caught off-guard and unprepared. Those are really the only choices we have.

One thing is clear. There are not enough police, firefighters, doctors and nurses, and other first responders to deal with multiple disasters in our country or around the world. Citizens must be prepared. They must be shown how to take care of themselves and each other.

Federal, state and county emergency services must be linked together efficiently and an effective chain of command put in place. Non-profit resources must be coordinated. And this is just the beginning of what needs to happen for an effective response to disaster. Preventing disaster requires a whole different effort.

The world we are living in requires a total shifting of our priorities in order to create safety for people who will be affected by earth changes, terrorism and deadly new diseases. We human beings can no longer afford to pour our resources into making war on each other. Those resources are going to be needed to provide care to the victims of a planetary wide upheaval.

We need to re-examine the way we live and create. We have created many products that do not contribute to our well-being or our survival. We even make products that harm us and endanger our lives. That, my friends, must stop. If we are engaged in making such products, purchasing them, or buying stock in the companies that make them, we must stop. We must carefully review what we support with our energy, our time, our attention, or our money. In the future, we must support only those products and services that bring a blessing to us, to our family, and to our planet.

Divine Mother is asking us to live in a way that is congruent with the values we hold. She is asking us not to engage in work that exploits others or that helps to create a bigger gap between rich and poor. She is asking us to use our career to help, to encourage, to support, to uplift. Divine Mother is asking us to care for Her children. If we don't do it, who will?

Divine Mother is asking us to stand up for what we believe. She wants our voice to be heard and our actions noted in our community. We are the beacon of light that must shine on inequality and injustice. Because we bring the light, all manner of trespass and abuse are exposed. Victims are spared more suffering, perpetrators come to justice, and atonement becomes possible.

Without our dedication, without our willingness to serve, the cries of Mother's children will not be heard. Without our efforts, a better, a kinder, and a saner world cannot be built.

Like our Divine Parents, we are creators. It is our nature to express who we are. It is our nature to share, to proclaim, to build. But we must not engage in the act of creation before we have allowed love to make its home in our heart, or what we create will not be helpful.

If we create, we must create only with love. We must create what is good for us and good for others. We must create that which fosters oneness and equality. We must create in a heartfelt manner and care responsibly for our creations.

We must not leave the job of caring to others. It is and must be our number one job. Lest we care, all of this is for naught.

One person can make a difference when he raises his voice up with conviction and stands as an example for others. Gandhi taught us that. Martin Luther King showed us the achievements of a great heart and an inspired mind. Mother Teresa showed us the power of one woman opposed to poverty and suffering.

We mustn't think that we are not up to the task. Divine Mother asks us to follow in their footsteps.

Whether we remember signing up or not, we volunteered some time ago to be in God's Army of Love Givers. We told God "Please use me," and now God is calling Her chips in.

Nero may have fiddled while Rome burned, but our fiddle is broken. We had better throw it in the fire and saddle up our horses. We have work to do here.

Recruitment Strategies

There are a lot of people on the planet and a lot of hearts and minds to be transformed. So what exactly is God's strategy for reaching them?

Guess what? S/He has chosen you to be one of the generals and chief recruiters. You get to enroll your own regiment.

"How do I do that?" you probably want to know.

Fortunately, it's not as hard as you think. You just start an Affinity Group of ten people. You create a real heart space filled with love and support for members. And then ten weeks later each one of those members goes out and starts his or her own Affinity Group of ten people.

Now you have a community of 100 people all being nurtured and supported. Once per week, you bring all Affinity Group members together for an interfaith healing service. This spiritual family of 100 people is the prototype building block for the creation of the houses of healing in your city or town.

Granted this takes real commitment and work. But it can be done within a year. And then let's say that this group of one hundred people begin to gather weekly in a large public hall that is open to people of all faiths who want to come and receive the Divine Love healing energies. Gradually, week by week, the group will grow as people go out and spread the word about the miracles and the healings that happen in this place.

By the end of the second year, attendance at the Interfaith Affinity Service should double or triple. It could even grow tenfold. At that point, anyone living in the larger community will begin to feel the divine love energy. The whole community will light up. People will be transformed by the power of love and guided to begin building the houses of healing that are most needed in that community.

Now you are just one person, but right now you can go out and find nine other people to join your group. Right now you can bring the healing balm of Divine Mother's energy to your community.

If you are wise, you will choose strong people from different backgrounds, different races, and different religions to join your group. That way each one of you will have the potential to reach back into powerful communities, each with its own center of influence. As a result, your larger community will be diverse and multifaceted. It will truly represent a cross-section of the people in your city or town.

The Affinity Process and the Laws of Love principles can also be taken into businesses and companies, government agencies, schools, hospitals, prisons, nursing homes and other institutions. It can be used to help people communicate with greater compassion and build work relationships based on acceptance and mutual respect.

There are no limits as to where these powerful principles and practices, and the healing energies resulting from them, can go. Indeed, you are the one who will know where to take the contents of this book and the previous two mastery volumes. For you will be guided to use these tools in a unique way that helps you to continue to heal and express your gifts.

You will also be guided to connect with others with complementary talents and skills. They will help you build this work.

None of this requires great brilliance or a Herculean effort on your part. It simply requires your willingness to show up and do the work that unfolds before you.

That is what it means to surrender to the will of God and to become the instrument of Her love and compassion in the world. There is no greater purpose than this available to you or anyone else. It will bring many blessings and rewards, as well as opportunities that you cannot imagine now.

New Jerusalem

The City of God cannot be built with our fear or our guilt. We must walk through our fears and atone for our guilt before we lay a single stone.

Otherwise, we will re-create the world of struggle and strife that we have now. In the New Jerusalem, gentile and Jew, Israeli and Palestinian must live in equality and peace.

So before we create, let us atone for our sins and forgive our trespasses. Let us atone today and each day of our lives. Let us acknowledge our mistakes and learn from them so that we do not repeat them.

Let us be clear in our hearts before we lay a single stone. Only what we build with love will endure throughout the vicissitudes of history. Only what we give in a loving way will be helpful to our children and our children's children.

The City of God, in truth, is not a place on planet Earth. It is a place in our hearts. When we dwell in that place, heaven is here; heaven is now. And the only thing that is revealed to us is what we already know.

In this moment, we are either loving each other or calling out for love. We always have that choice. Even in the final moment, when the last human being takes her last breath, she will have that choice.

Until then, let us cultivate hope and have the courage to express our gifts. Until the jury returns with its verdict on the human experiment, let us work and pray without ceasing for equality, justice and peace. Let us be the bringers of love to ourselves and to each other. Let us be the presence of love in each moment.

Together, we can make the world a better place. We can assist in the collective shift of human consciousness from fear to love.

Because of our compassionate service, a golden age can be created on Planet Earth. We can learn to take care of all our people. Poverty, crime and weapons of mass destruction can disappear. People can learn to serve the greater good and treat each other as equals.

The Kingdom of God can be created on earth. And our planet can once again shine in the heavens as a place of peace, a place where all can come to take refuge and experience the healing power of unconditional love.

May it be so. May this be our work, now and in the times to come!

Namaste,

Paul Ferrini

APPENDIX ONE:

Summary of Spiritual Mastery Principles

Students in the Spiritual Mastery program are working with the principles and practices presented in *The Laws of Love* and *The Power of Love* books. Here is what they are learning:

1. They are learning to connect with God in the silence of their hearts. They are in daily communion with their Source and they are beginning to embody the energy of unconditional love.

2. They are learning to see and treat others as equals. They are aware that none of their judgments are justified and each one must be lovingly forgiven. They are beginning to understand that their good and the good of others is one and the same.

3. They are learning to look at their shadow and to bring it into the light. They understand that, whenever their buttons are pushed, they are being asked to love and accept some part of themselves they have denied or rejected. They are integrating the wounded child and the spiritual adult.

4. They are learning to manifest what they care about and are committed to. They are willing to do all that is necessary to care for their loved ones and bring their dreams into reality.

5. They are learning not to give their power away to others or to be victims. They are beginning to realize that their lives are the reflection of the choices that they make and they are learning to choose more wisely.

6. They are learning to feel compassion for others. They know

that all human beings have the same hurts and struggles and they are reaching out to others in their community, creating a safe space for healing and empowerment.

7. They are refining their skills and talents and developing the confidence to give their gifts to the world. They are beginning to step forward as creative people, as teachers, healers, leaders and role models for others.

8. They are beginning to heal their emotional wounds and to reach out to others with similar wounds. They see how their gifts and talents can be used to facilitate healing for themselves and others.

9. They are learning to accept themselves fully as unique individuals. They are giving themselves permission to be who they are and granting others the same freedom. They live with clear boundaries and mutual respect for others.

10. They are learning to live in the world without being caught up in the drama. Peace and harmony prevail in their lives, as they learn to keep things simple and celebrate the little things that make them feel close to nature and to God.

Perhaps you have learned the same lessons by following another spiritual practice or simply by allowing life to teach you directly. If so, congratulations! There are many footpaths up the mountain. This *Course* is only one of them.

Whatever path you have traveled, you would not be knocking on this door if you had not already learned to walk with an open heart and an open mind. You would not be here if your hands were not extended outward to others.

APPENDIX TWO:

Information on the Spiritual Mastery Program

Shifting Your Life Through One Year of Practice

Thirty plus years of heart-centered spiritual work have taught me what is necessary to bring about a real, lasting change in consciousness and experience. I have designed this one-year intensive program in spiritual mastery to give you the experience and support that you need to wake up without having to abandon your present lifestyle.

However, that does not mean that your life will continue on automatic pilot. Many changes will result from your one-year commitment to spiritual practice. The shift will happen first on the inside and then on the outside, as the rest of your life comes into alignment with the new energy that you learn to embody. By the end of the year, everything that is not in harmony with the truth of your essence will begin to fall away. For most this will be a gentle and gradual process.

In the course of your year of training, you will begin to discover your life purpose and begin actively pursuing it. You will start following your bliss, expressing your talents and abilities and helping others to heal and to grow.

You will also begin actively healing your family of origin wounds, along with the unworthiness attached to them. You will relinquish victim consciousness, abandon shame and blame, and be actively creating relationships of mutual love and acceptance. If you are married, you will bring a deeper love and understanding to your partner. If you are single, you will understand how to create a spiritual relationship. You may even attract your life partner or soul mate.

Regardless of the form it takes, you will be connected to love and love will take charge of your life. When fear comes up, which it will do from time to time, you will hold it gently and compassionately.

You will be true to who you are and accepting of others the way they are. You will be a love-bringer and a peacemaker. You will help to make the world a better place. You will actively assist in the collective shift of human consciousness from fear to love.

Below are the three components of the *Spiritual Mastery Training Program.*

One: Immersion in the Container Energy

After reading the three books in the *Spiritual Mastery* series, the next step in the *Mastery* process is to attend a retreat. This enables you to experience the divine love energy and begin to anchor it in your heart. You will be attending at least four retreats over the course of your training. Each retreat will enable you to experience this energy more deeply and to understand how to commune with it and let it guide your life.

Two: Support and Ongoing Healing

In between retreats you will receive weekly support from your spiritual community. Your peers will be emotionally present for you and you for them as you learn to integrate your retreat experience and the spiritual mastery principles and practices into your daily life. Some will elect to receive weekly spiritual counseling or coaching from me or from another staff member. Tele-seminars and Affinity Groups by phone will be available to you to help you stay connected.

Three: Extension and Community Building

Every time you return from a retreat, you will be asked to give back the energy you received to people in your community. One of the ways that you stay connected to the presence of love is by giving love to others. The community will support you in meeting the challenges you face in stepping into your leadership role. By the end of the year you will be helping to create a house of healing for those who have experienced trauma/life lessons similar to your own. You will become a leader and a force for healing and reconciliation in your community

***

If you are interested in participating in the Spiritual Mastery Program, I invite you to write to me. Please share with me your life experience and your spiritual direction. Tell me what your needs are and how you think this program might meet them.

Paul Ferrini, Heartways Press
9 Phillips St. Greenfield, MA 01301
info@heartwayspress.com

APPENDIX THREE

Workbook Lessons for each Chapter for Mastery Students and Teachers

Week One: Introduction

As you read this Chapter, give some thought to the following questions, reflect on them in your journal, and come to class prepared to share your experiences with others.

How do you see the old world breaking down around you? What no longer works in your life? What changes in your life is Spirit asking you to make, so that you can take off your mask or your straightjacket and begin living a more natural and empowered life that honors you fully?

Please articulate your positive vision for the future of your life.

Week Two: The Presence of Love (Chapter 1)

Every day this week, practice this meditation.

Allow yourself to get quiet and to feel the Presence of Love in your heart. Feel it as a warmth, a vibration, a palpable energetic reality. Using the breath, extend the Presence until it dwells in every cell of your body, in every feeling and thought that you have. Let the Presence of Love fill you up completely, and then let it extend out to all of the people in your life, embracing them, affirming them, accepting them just the way that they are. Be in the cocoon of Love energy. Trust the spiritual wings within you as your heart opens and you are uplifted into grace. Feel the Divine Love energy as a new energetic ground of being, a new existential reality.

When you are embodying the Divine Love energy, you are no longer the caterpillar caught in chrysalis, but the bright butterfly fluttering from flower to flower. You are no longer just a human but a human being on fire with Spirit, divinely blessed, divinely guided and inspired.

Do this meditation every day when you wake up until your feel the Divine Love energy, the Presence of Love, dwelling fully in your heart.

During the week, do not dwell on the past or the future. Let yourself be rooted consciously in the present moment. Sink your roots deeply into the ground. Do not be distracted by memories of the past or expectations of the future. Let them come and go, without being attached to them. Just as the leaves of the tree return to rest after the wind has stirred them, let your heart be still and your mind be open.

Bring all of yourself into the present moment.

Realize that you do not know anything and experience the freedom of not having to know. Be with what is. You don't have to analyze it or interpret it or know what it means. Just be present with it. Accept it. Embrace it with love.

Reflect on these practices in your journal and come to class prepared to share your experiences with others.

Week Three: The Call to Awaken (Chapter 2)

This week, please address the following questions in your journal and come to class prepared to share your answers.

When and how in your life have you heard the call of Spirit? What is it calling you to be or to do? Have you answered the call yet? If not, what is holding you back? What support do you need to step forward and play your part in the healing of human consciousness on planet earth?

In order to help you hear and trust the call of Spirit, say the Spiritual Mastery prayer with conviction at least once per day every day this week. See how new opportunities open up this week for you to heal, to step into your power, and to help others heal. Consider how the Divine Being is responding to your offer to heal and to serve.

Week Four: Messages from the Masters (Chapter 3)

As you read the Messages from the Masters in this chapter, did you feel energy in your heart, in your hands, in your feet, or in other places in your body? Did you feel a warmth, a vibration, a resonance? If so, understand that this is an energetic recognition of the rightness of the material and its profound importance to you. It means that you are being called to serve. You can no longer sit on the sidelines and watch. You are a participant in the uplifting of human consciousness on planet Earth.

If it is possible for you to join an Affinity Group, participate in a teleconference, or to come to a retreat, consider making the commitment now. Being with others of like mind helps to anchor in the Divine Love energy so that it can guide and direct your life. Let the energy move you to act for your highest good in a timely manner.

Reflect in your journal about any specific messages that moved you and come to class prepared to share your experiences.

Week Five: Divine Mother (Chapter 4)

As you read through this chapter, reflect on your experience with Divine Mother. Have you been able to connect with Her unconditional love in your heart? Have you been able to create a safe space of loving acceptance for yourself and others in your life?

This week, practice Mother's teaching of acceptance and not-fixing. Accept your life as it is. Accept others as they are. When you see yourself trying to fix someone, be aware of it, and remind yourself that you are not here to fix anyone.

Consider how your relationship with Divine Mother is different from your relationship with God the Father. Does it make it easier or harder for you to relate to God as female?

What was the nature of your relationship with your mother? Did you have an absent or overbearing mother? What is your mother wound and how have you begun to heal it? How has that wound affected your relationship with spouse, children and significant others?

Please reflect on these questions in your journal and come to class prepared to share your thoughts, feelings and experiences.

Week Six: Divine Father (Chapter 5)

As you read this chapter, please reflect on your experience of the Father energy. Did you grow up with a dominant, abusive, absent or unavailable father? What wounds were created as a result of your experience with your father and other significant men in your life? How have you begin to heal from those wounds and to what extent do they continue to run your life in negative ways?

Have you received the mentoring and encouragement you need to trust your talents, develop your skills, and express your gifts? If not, how can you find positive male role models to assist you?

Are you supporting yourself and your family financially? Are you doing work that you love? Are you fulfilling your life purpose? If not, how can you begin to heal your father wound so that you can empower and express yourself fully?

Please reflect on these questions in your journal and come to class prepared to share your thoughts, feelings and experiences.

Week Seven: Divine Guidance (Chapter 6)

Does your spiritual practice enable you to connect to God and to receive Divine Guidance on the important matters of your life? Do you trust your guidance and act on it? In what aspect of your life are you resisting the guidance you have received?

Are you doing your daily and weekly spiritual practices and seeing steady benefits or is your practice sporadic? Will you chop wood, carry water, and clean the latrines, if necessary, or are you looking for special treatment?

Are you humble and teachable? Are you willing to do your human apprenticeship and learn the lessons of the Earth plane? Can you be patient with your own awakening process or do you need to get there in a hurry?

Please reflect on these questions in your journal and come to class prepared to share your thoughts, feelings and experiences.

Week Eight: The Call of the Children (Chapter 7)

If you have children, how are they doing? Are they empowered and successful or are they struggling to survive? Are they able to work and/or go to school, or do they feel alienated and cut off from society? Whether or not you have children, do you feel the pain of young people and hear their cry for help? If so, are you guided to answer the call?

Have you or someone close to you ever been sexually abused? Has the abuse been acknowledged? Has the shame and the anger come up for healing? Have you forgiven yourself? Have you forgiven the perpetrator? Have you moved on or does this wound continue to hold you back in your life? Are you willing to reach out to others who can help you heal your wound? Are you willing to help others heal?

If these two houses of healing don't speak to you, which ones do? Where have you been most deeply wounded? What house of healing do you need to help build so that you and others like you can get the support and empowerment you need? How can your greatest talents and gifts be used?

Please reflect on these questions in your journal and come to class prepared to share your thoughts, feelings and experiences.

Week Nine: The Real Revelation (Chapter 8)

How do you feel about the times that we are living in? Are you scared? Do you feel powerless to do anything? Are you afraid that humans are being punished by an angry God? Do you think that we have the will, the time, and the resources to solve our collective problems or do you think it's too little too late? And how does this belief impact your willingness to step forward and get involved as a healer and change agent in these challenging times?

Do you see the seeds of violence in yourself? Do you see how the same seeds are planted in every mind and heart? Do you see how they grow and out-picture in the collective consciousness?

How can you uproot the seeds of violence in your own life? How can you turn your knives into tuning forks and your swords into ploughshares? How does your healing from your wounds and traumas affect the healing of the collective heart and mind?

Please reflect on these questions in your journal and come to class prepared to share your thoughts, feelings and experiences.

Week Ten: The New Jerusalem (Chapter 9)

Take some time this week and write down your vision of the kind of world that you would like to create on planet Earth. Be as specific as you can be and be clear about how your gifts can be used to help manifest your vision.

Come to the group ready to share your vision.

One at a time, let everyone in the group put her vision up on newsprint. Once the vision is shared, let everyone in the group offer encouragement and support to that person in manifesting her vision.

After all have shared their individual visions, identify those components of the visions that are held in common. Write these components down on a separate sheet of newsprint. Then, write a mission statement for the group incorporating these components. Agree to meet together again to support each other's individual visions and to develop strategies to manifest the group's common vision.

Paul Ferrini is the author of over 30 books on love, healing and forgiveness. His unique blend of radical Christianity and other wisdom traditions goes beyond self-help and recovery into the heart of healing. His conferences, retreats, and *Affinity Group Process* have helped thousands of people deepen their practice of forgiveness and open their hearts to the divine presence in themselves and others.

For more information on Paul's work, visit the web-site at *www.paulferrini.com,* email: info@**heartwayspress.com** or write to **Heartways Press, 9 Phillips Steet, Greenfield, MA 01301.**

New Releases from Heartways Press

Paul Ferrini's *Course in Spiritual Mastery*

Part One: The Laws of Love
A Guide to Living in Harmony
with Universal Spiritual Truth
144 pages $12.95
ISBN # 1-879159-60-0

Part Two: The Power of Love
10 Spiritual Practices that Can Transform
Your Life
168 pages $12.95
ISBN # 1-879159-61-9

Part Three: The Presence of Love
God's Answer to Humanity's Call for Help
160 pages $12.95
ISBN # 1-879159-62-7

Paul's In-depth Presentation of the Laws of Love on 9 CDs

THE LAWS OF LOVE
Part One (5 CDs) ISBN # 1-879159-58-9 $49.00
Part Two (4 CDs) ISBN # 1-879159-59-7 $39.00

Audio Workshops on CD

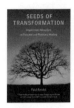

Seeds of Transformation:
5 cd set includes: Healing Without Fixing, The Wound and the Gift, Opening to the Divine Love Energy, The Laws of Love, The Path to Mastery.
5 CDs   ISBN 1-879159-63-5 $48.00

Two Talks on Spiritual Mastery
by Paul Ferrini
We are the Bringers of Love   CD 1
Surrendering to What Is   CD 2
2 CDs   ISBN 1-879159-65-1 $24.00

Love is That Certainty
ISBN 1-879159-52-X $16.95

Atonement: The Awakening of Planet Earth and its Inhabitants
ISBN 1-879159-53-8 $16.95

From Darkness to Light:
The Soul's Journey of Redemption
ISBN 1-879159-54-6 $16.95

Relationship Books

Dancing with the Beloved: Opening our
Hearts to the Lessons of Love
ISBN 1-879159-47-3
160 pages paperback $12.95

Living in the Heart:
The Affinity Process and the Path of
Unconditional Love and Acceptance
128 pages paperback ISBN 1-879159-36-8
$10.95

Creating a Spiritual Relationship
128 pages paperback
ISBN 1-879159-39-2 $10.95

The Twelve Steps of Forgiveness
120 pages paperback ISBN 1-879159-10-4
$10.95

The Ecstatic Moment:
A Practical Manual for Opening Your Heart
and Staying in It.
128 pages   paperback   ISBN 1-879159-18-X
$10.95

Christ Mind Books

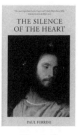

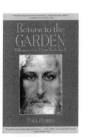

Part 1   Part 2   Part 3   Part 4

Love Without Conditions ISBN 1-879159-15-5 $12.00
The Silence of the Heart ISBN 1-879159-16-3 $14.95
Miracle of Love ISBN 1-879159-23-6 $12.95
Return to the Garden   ISBN 1-879159-35-x $12.95

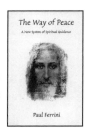

The Living Christ ISBN 1-879159-49-X paperback $14.95
I am the Door hardcover ISBN 1-879159-41-4 $21.95
The Way of Peace hardcover ISBN 1-879159-42-2 $19.95
Reflections of the Christ Mind hardcover $19.95

Wisdom Books and Audio

Everyday Wisdom
A Spiritual Book of Days
224 pages paperback $13.95
ISBN 1-879159-51-1

Wisdom Cards: Spiritual Guidance
for Every Day of our Lives
ISBN 1-879159-50-3 $10.95
*Each full color card features a beautiful
painting evoking an archetypal theme*

Forbidden Fruit: Unraveling the Mysteries
of Sin, Guilt and Atonement
ISBN 1-879159-48-1
160 pages paperback $12.95

Enlightenment for Everyone
with an Introduction by Iyanla Vanzant
ISBN 1-879159-45-7
160 pages hardcover $16.00

The Great Way of All Beings:
Renderings of Lao Tzu
ISBN 1-879159-46-5
320 pages hardcover $23.00

Grace Unfolding: The Art
of Living A Surrendered Life
96 pages   paperback   ISBN 1-879159-37-6 $9.95

Illuminations on the Road to Nowhere
160 pages   paperback
ISBN 1-879159-44-9 $12.95

Audio Books

The Economy of Love Readings from *Silence of the Heart,*
The Ecstatic Moment, Grace Unfolding and other books.
ISBN 1-879159-56-2 $16.95

Relationship as a Spiritual Path Readings from *Creating a*
Spiritual Relationship, Dancing with the Beloved, Miracle of Love and other
books. ISBN 1-879159-55-4 $16.95

The Hands of God Readings from *Illuminations, Enlightenment*
for Everyone, Forbidden Fruit, The Great Way of All Beings and other
books. ISBN 1-879159-57-0 $16.95

Love Without Conditions Read by the author, 3 CDs.
3.25 hours ISBN 1-879159-64-3 $36.00
Also available on cassette tape for $19.95

Order any of these products on our website:
www.paulferrini.com

or call toll free in the US: 1-888-HARTWAY

The website has many excerpts from
Paul Ferrini's books, as well as information
on his workshops and retreats.

Be sure to request Paul's free email newsletter,
his inspirational weekly wisdom message,
and a free catalog of his books
and audio products.

Heartways Press
9 Phillips Street
Greenfield, MA 01301
413-774-9474   Fax: 413-774-9475
www.heartwayspress.com
email: info@heartwayspress.com.